Introduction..........

Prayer...................

I Just Want to Be Her 6
The Story Unfolds.. 9

A Star is Born.. 12
You'll See... 16
Surprise Surprise.. 20

Because You Made Me Mad.. 25
Misunderstandings... 29
The Thorntons.. 33

The Gift.. 37
The Sanctuary.. 40
The Healing.. 44

Outside Looking In... 48
Hidden Eclipse... 53
Blending the Right Way... 56

Piece of My Heart.. 60
Wonder Woman... 64
The Amazing Michael Jackson.. 67

Ear Infection to Eulogy.. 71
Grief: The Uninvited Guest... 75
Stages of Aging.. 78

The Glorious Homegoing... 82
A Home Built on Faith... 86
Imposter Syndrome.. 90

Menopause: The Mysterious Club... 93

Healing in the Hands of a Stranger 97
The Unexpected Journey 100

To My New Family 108
Real Love and Real Lessons 111
Epilogue: Embracing the Journey 114

Prayer 117
A Challenge to You 118

Dedication

To Kelcey, my "Baby Diddy,"—thank you for being my constant cheerleader, prayer warrior, and partner. Your unwavering support of my "projects," your willingness to listen to my stories, and your laughter at my jokes mean more to me than words can express. You make my life lighter, brighter, and full of love.

To my daughters and sons—you are my heart walking outside my body. My love for you is endless, and I am endlessly grateful to be your favorite girl.

To my grands—being your "Shooby" and "Nana" is the most incredible honor of my life. You fill my world with joy and purpose, and I adore every moment I share with you.

To my friends—thank you for the laughter, the love, the support, and the steadfast presence.

You all give me stories worth writing, jokes worth telling, and a life worth celebrating. This book is for all of you…my heart and my inspiration.

Introduction

Life has a way of writing its own stories, doesn't it? Stories we never planned for, moments we couldn't have scripted, and lessons we didn't know we needed. If someone had told me years ago that I would one day put my life on display for the world to read, I would've laughed, a deep, belly-shaking laugh—the kind that leaves you slapping your friend's arm and fills rooms to leave echoes. Yet here I am, inviting you into my life's colorful, messy, laughter-filled tapestry.

This is not a story about perfection. Lord knows I've made my share of mistakes—probably more than my share—but it is a story about love, growth, and finding joy in the journey. From the chaos of raising a blended family of six children to the quiet moments spent nurturing my many plants, my life has been a constant ebb and flow of laughter, tears, and lessons. I've learned that some of the best teachers aren't in classrooms; they're found in relationships, failures, triumphs, and even the tiny, seemingly insignificant moments we often overlook.

This collection of stories is me offering you a chance to sit with me for a while—perhaps with your favorite cup of coffee or tea in hand—and laugh, cry, and reflect together. You'll meet the people who have shaped me, the challenges that have refined me, and the love that has sustained me. You'll walk with me through my quirks and contradictions, victories and valleys, and perhaps see reflections of your own life along the way.

So please pull up a chair, settle in, and share in this moment. I pray that these stories will remind you that there is beauty even in life's unpredictability. Even in the broken places, there is hope. Even when the journey feels long, you never walk it alone. Here's to the laughter, the love, the lessons, and the joy of discovering who we're meant to be.

A Prayer for the Journey

Lord,

As we open these pages, I invite Your presence into this space and the readers' lives. Thank You for the gift of storytelling, for weaving joy and sorrow, love and lessons, into the fabric of our lives. May these stories, though imperfect, reflect Your grace and the beauty of the journey You've set before each of us. Bless the hearts and minds of those who read this book.

May they find laughter that lifts their spirits and heals like medicine. May they uncover love that reminds them of their worth and lessons that guide them forward. Let them see glimpses of You in the triumphs and the trials, in the quiet moments and the loud ones, in the laughter and even in the tears.

Help us all embrace the messiness of life with gratitude and humility, knowing that every step—even the stumbling ones—leads us closer to the purpose You've designed for us. May this book be a gentle reminder that none of us walks alone and that in every season, Your hand is steady and sure.

Thank You for the gift of connection, the power of shared experiences, and the hope we find in You. Bless this journey, Lord, and bless every person who walks it with me.

In Jesus's name,

Amen.

I Just Want to be Her

There is a woman in my life who has always been there for me—steadfast and unwavering, no matter what I faced. To be honest, I haven't always been kind to her. I didn't treat her the way she deserved, yet she consistently showed up for me, handling everything with a grace I often took for granted. She's been there my whole life, but for a long time, I ignored her advice. She's incredibly intelligent, with a sense of humor that can light up the darkest days. She laughs in the face of chaos and finds silver linings in storms that would send most people running for cover. And yet, when she would gently warn me about people or situations, I dismissed her—even though her intentions were always pure, always for my good.

I know what you're thinking: How could I treat someone so devoted to me so poorly? Believe me, I ask myself the same question, but I need you to know—I've changed. Back then, there were moments when she'd watch me vent my frustrations with friends who ignored my advice, and I know she was thinking, Hmm, sound familiar? But she never judged me, even when I was hard on her. I told her she wasn't good enough. That she was too fat, too dark, too silly. I told her no one would ever take her seriously. I yelled at her for loving people who didn't deserve her, for forgiving people who hurt her "all in the name of the Lord." All the while, she kept trying to teach me to love her, even as I doubted her worth. I'll admit, I let the mistreatment from others shape how I treated her. I didn't trust her, didn't trust what she was trying to show me. And I didn't fight for her when she needed me. When people hurt her—called her names or tore her down—I stood by in silence. I failed her in ways that still sting when I think about it.

But one day, as I reflected on the people who walked away and the few who stayed, I realized something profound: she never left. Through it all, she stood at the forefront, shoulder-to-shoulder with Jesus, loving me in a way I didn't always deserve. She saw me as He did: beautifully flawed but priceless. Always enough. Now, with the wisdom life has taught me, I listen to her voice above all others. I trust her judgment, and I love her as fiercely as she loves me. I've learned to see her through God's eyes, to appreciate the way she roots for me, believes in me, and shows up for me every single day. She wants the best for me and sees the best in me. And I can honestly say, I love her—completely. I love her flaws and her strengths. I love her ability to love others so freely, without judgment. I love how she always seeks to understand the feelings of others, including my own. Her emotional intelligence is unmatched because she genuinely loves her neighbor as herself.

She is me. I am her.
I just want to be her…to embrace her resilience, her kindness, her heart…to stand in her strength and walk in her grace.

Every single day, I JUST WANT TO BE HER.

The Story Unfolds

One lazy afternoon, I sat listening to the soft whimpers of my grandson, Khyson. It was one of those moments when gratitude sneaks up on you and warms your heart from the inside out. I couldn't help but marvel at the privilege of being alive to witness my rainbow baby, Santana, bringing her own rainbow baby into the world. From the moment I heard the news of her pregnancy, my mind raced with visions of what life would look like when Khyson arrived. Would he have Santana's tenacity or her boundless determination? Every waking thought revolved around how I could ensure this child—my legacy—would never go without. Then, as if God had decided my hands weren't full enough, Santana gave birth to Kashton exactly one year and one day later. Yes, two grandsons now living under my roof, each with their own unique way of filling the house with equal parts chaos and joy.

Suddenly, my to-do list felt longer than a CVS receipt, and one thing became glaringly clear: I needed money, and Lord, I needed it yesterday! As the boys giggled in the background, oblivious to my financial musings, I began to brainstorm ways to create stability for my growing family. How could I maximize my time and generate more income to provide the life these boys—and their mama—deserved? The suggestions poured in from well-meaning friends and family:
"You should do stand-up comedy. You're hilarious!"
"You'd make a fantastic motivational speaker. People would flock to hear you."
"Your life is wild enough for a reality TV show!"
"What about writing devotionals for teachers? Your words are so uplifting."

The ideas ranged from practical to downright absurd, but each one hinted at the same truth: My life, as dramatic and unpredictable as it was, held stories worth sharing. After a few conversations with trusted advisors (and some hard laughs at the reality TV idea), the lightbulb finally went off. I needed to put my life on paper. Now, let me be real with you. I'm a little extra—a sprinkle of flair on a plain bagel, if you will. When I tell stories, people often raise an eyebrow, wondering if I've embellished the details. But here's the kicker: I don't need to. My life is that dramatic. I'm convinced it would give the most scripted soap operas a run for their money.

This memoir won't be ordinary. It's not a dry recounting of dates and milestones but a vibrant tapestry of the weirdest, funniest, and most unexpected moments that life has thrown my way. I mean, sure, maybe everyone's life has its quirks, but I've yet to meet someone whose everyday chaos rivals mine. (Lol!) What you're about to read is a colorful, no-holds-barred journey through my life—the twists, turns, and laugh-out-loud moments that shaped me into the woman I am today. These pages represent my unapologetic embrace of me. Methany. A woman who has learned to stand tall in her identity, at an astounding four feet eleven inches tall, who doesn't want to be anyone else but herself.

So buckle up. This ride is going to be full of heart, humor, and a few curveballs. I don't know where life will take me next, but one thing's for sure: I don't want to be anyone else. I just want to be her. Enjoy!

A Star Is Born

This is my very dramatic yet loving version of how I made my grand entrance into the world. Now, I can't promise that every detail is accurate, but thanks to the bits and pieces of family lore I've gathered and my sanctified imagination, I've crafted this story just for your enjoyment. (Insert time machine chimes here.)

The table is set like something out of a Southern Living magazine, except with more soul and flavor. The finest linen drapes the surface, and each place setting shines with fancy dishes and silverware polished to perfection. The centerpiece? A feast fit for royalty: roasted turkey, pineapple-glazed ham, fried chicken, macaroni and cheese bubbling with cheesy goodness, candied yams dripping with butter, cinnamon, and brown sugar, collard greens cooked just right, and golden cornbread slathered in butter. Mommee strides in from the kitchen, carefully balancing a tray with banana pudding and a decadent red velvet cake, the final touch to a masterpiece.

Mommee, a vision of grace despite her limp, wears a blue muumuu scattered with cheerful yellow daisies. Her long black hair, a nod to her Native American roots, is tied neatly back, and her smile—oh, that smile—lights up the room. But don't let her sweetness fool you; she runs her household like a well-oiled machine. Today, her apron hangs loose around her neck, signaling a big event: company is coming. "Snook," she calls, her voice soft but commanding. Daddee saunters in, towering and broad, with hands so big they could palm a basketball like a toy. His usual grizzly scowl is slightly softened by the thought of seeing the grands—his beloved grandkids. While he's not exactly thrilled about the "company," the grands have a way of pulling out his rare, deep-throated laugh that sounds like an ebony Santa Claus.

"Irene," he grumbles, "how much longer we gotta wait?"

Mommee waves him off with a smile. "Just need to add the flowers," she replies, as if the blooms will complete the symphony she's orchestrated. He responds with a playful smack on her bottom, pulling her into a quick bear hug before they're interrupted by a knock at the door. The family begins to trickle in, filling the house with laughter and the clamor of little feet. Buck, Lou, Wilma, Tim, Titus, Nita, Mary, and Trenia arrive with their families, their hugs and chatter a warm balm to the chilly November air. Another knock heralds Jeannie's entrance, her round belly leading the way as little Chris and Dink toddle behind her.

Daddee scoops up Chris and Dink, racing through the house like a freight train, their squeals of joy echoing through the halls. Mommee greets everyone with her signature warmth, saving Jeannie for last. She bends to kiss Jeannie's belly, whispering sweet words of anticipation to the life stirring within. Amid the chaos, Jeannie retreats to the den for a quick nap, her peace-sign shirt stretched taut over her belly and complemented by a plaid mini-skirt and white go-go boots. Her burgundy afro is a crown of confidence, though she hides her dazzling smile, self-conscious about the brown tooth she earned defending her sister in a fight.

Her nap is abruptly cut short by a sharp pain. Clutching her abdomen, she meets Mommee's knowing eyes. "You alright, baby?" Mommee asks, her voice a soothing balm. Jeannie nods weakly, and they shuffle to the dining room, where the family has gathered around the table, their chatter a symphony of gratitude. As the family shares what they're thankful for, Jeannie grimaces through the waves of pain. She manages to smile and tells everyone how grateful she is to be surrounded by her loved ones. Daddee, overcome with emotion, leads the family in a thunderous prayer of thanks, his voice booming with love and gratitude.

Before the "amen" can even echo, Jeannie's water breaks. The room erupts into chaos. Tim bolts outside to start the car. Nita and Wilma help Jeannie to her feet while Mary and Trenia volunteer to stay behind with the grands, secretly eyeing the untouched feast.

At Erlanger Hospital, the nurses usher Jeannie into the labor room, with Mommee moving faster than anyone thought possible. An hour later, Mommee cradles a tiny bundle with bushy curls, skin the color of a pinto bean, and wise, bright eyes that seem to take in the world with an old soul's curiosity. In the nursery, the nurse looks up to see the entire family—grands included—pressed against the glass, their collective love radiating through the room. Dink tugs on Daddee's hand and asks, "What's her name, Daddee?" Wilma answers with a smile, "Her name is Methany."

Mommee, beaming with pride, declares, "On this Thanksgiving Day, November 27, 1975, a star is born. And one day, she's gonna be somebody." Turns out, Mommee was right.

You'll See

Fast forward from Thanksgiving 1975 to a crisp spring morning in 1980. I was four years old, groggy, and oblivious to the life-changing day ahead. Mama woke me up before the sun, her gentle touch pulling me from my dreams. She washed my face with a warm cloth, her movements tender but her eyes filled with an emotion I couldn't yet name. "Where are we going so early?" I mumbled, still half-asleep. "You'll see," she whispered, her voice heavy with something I didn't understand.

The mystery deepened when days later I saw my favorite dress draped over the rocking chair—the white one with tiny purple flowers. Excitement bubbled up. "Why am I getting so dressed up?" Mama looked at me, sadness pooling in her eyes. "You'll see." She helped me into the dress, followed by tiny white socks with lace and shiny black patent leather shoes. It was all so strange, yet I trusted her. Even as questions buzzed in my mind, I stayed quiet. But when I saw the tears slip from her eyes, I couldn't hold it in anymore. "Mama, what's wrong?" I asked softly. She placed her finger gently against my lips and said once more, "Met, you'll see."

Breakfast was different that morning. My brother and sisters were dressed up too, their faces somber and quiet. The usual chaos and laughter that filled our mornings were replaced with an eerie stillness. I fidgeted in my seat, desperate for answers, but no one was talking—not even to each other. As we piled into our old brown station wagon, I was thrilled to sit in my favorite spot: the trunk, where I could watch the world rush by. But not today. Mama buckled me into a seat. This was new. This was weird. WHAT IS GOING ON?! "Mama, where are we going?" She wiped her tears and said softly, "Methany, you'll see."

She called me by my full name. That's when I knew something was really wrong. "Are we going to see Mommee and Daddee?" I asked, hoping for something familiar.

No answer.

Fear crept over me. I hadn't seen Mommee or had our morning coffee chat in days. Our routine was sacred—her thick brown legs crossed as she rocked in her chair, her deep, husky voice sharing her thoughts on the world while I contributed the wisdom of a four-year-old. "Mama, is Mommee okay?" I whispered. She didn't reply. Instead, her tears flowed freely, and my heart clenched.

We arrived at a building with a parking lot crowded with cars. My stomach turned. This wasn't the comforting visit I'd imagined. Mama carried me inside, her arms tight around me as we walked through shiny blue floors and a long hallway filled with hushed murmurs. "I'm so sorry to hear about Irene," someone said. I tugged at Mama's arm. "Who's Irene?" "You'll see," she whispered again, her voice breaking.

The hallway opened into a room packed with people. I spotted my aunts, uncles, cousins—and there he was. "DADDEE!" I shouted, wriggling free from Mama's arms to run to him. His familiar bear hug calmed me, but his face was so sad. Why? Then I saw it: a long, silver box surrounded by flowers. "Mama, what's in that box?" Her voice trembled. "You'll see."

I stood on the seat to get a better look. And there she was. "MOMMEE!" I screamed. My little body shook with terror. "They got my Mommee in there! Get her out! Wake her up! It's time for coffee!" The room erupted into sobs, my family inconsolable. But I couldn't stop. I wailed, begging anyone who would listen to save her. The rest of the day passed in a blur, my mind unable to process what I had seen. When we returned home, I ran upstairs to her rocking chair, desperate for the comfort of her presence. And there she was. Mommee sat rocking, her face radiant with the smile I loved so much. I waved, tears streaming down my face. "Mama!" I shouted, running to get her.

Mama followed me upstairs, but when we reached the chair, it was empty. The chair still rocked gently, as if holding the memory of her. "She came to say goodbye," Mama whispered, pulling me into a tight hug. That night, I cried myself to sleep, clutching the memories of her scent, her laughter, and the way she made me feel so loved.

That day shaped me in ways I couldn't understand at the time. I hate surprises now; they make me anxious, always reminding me of that day. I've learned to ask questions, to prepare myself, to avoid being caught off guard. Even as a Christian, I struggled with waiting on God, often demanding answers and solutions right away. But life doesn't work like that, and neither does faith. Over the years, I've learned to trust God's timing, even when it's hard. Psalm 27:14 reminds me, "Wait on the Lord. Be of good courage, and He shall strengthen your heart."

Every time I read that verse, it feels like God is gently saying, "Methany… you'll see."

And now, I believe Him.

Surprise Surprise
(2019)

At the time I wrote *You'll See* about six years ago, I finally understood the root of my disdain for surprises. That childhood memory of seeing my "Mommee" in the casket still lingers, and every time I sense that something out of my control is about to happen, I feel the same heavy knot in my chest. Sometimes, it's intuition; most times, it's fear. I can't count the moments when surprise wasn't my friend. Take this for instance: I once got off work early and couldn't get my then-boyfriend to pick me up. He had my car, wasn't answering his phone, and my annoyance was growing. I hitched a ride home, and guess what I found? Him, his friend, and two young ladies *chilling*—like life was grand! Oh, I was LIVID. Did this incident add to my fear of surprises? Absolutely. But I don't just hate *bad* surprises. Nope. I hate them *all*. Even the dreaded "We need to talk" kind.

Now, let me tell you about one "surprise" I'll never forget. It was at my school district's annual kickoff event. Every year, the entire district gathers at the high school performing arts center to reflect on the previous year and gear up for the next. Teachers, staff, everyone. It's a whole thing. I showed up, grabbed breakfast, and hung out with some of my teacher friends in the parking lot. One of them, Yvette—our front office mama figure—came over and looped her arm through mine. "Sit with me today," she said, flashing a warm smile. "I need some extra support." I didn't think much of it. Of course, I'd sit with her!

The kickoff started with the usual: a video montage of students from the past year. We laughed, we got misty-eyed, all the feels. Then came the *"Be Somebody" Award*—a recognition of staff members who go above and beyond in extraordinary ways who are nominated by their principal or peers.

The video started with my friend Zandra saying something about "a huge bright spot in her day." Natalie chimed in, "When you hear the sound of her laugh, it's hard not to laugh; it's hard not to smile." Dayton, my former principal, described someone as "extremely positive... the kind of person who lifts up everyone in the room."

I sat there nodding along, guessing with my friends who it could be. *Definitely not me,* I thought. Chelsea added, "She inspires students and people every day... she's the teacher you want for your kids because she takes a special interest in them." By now, the people around me were looking my way, grinning knowingly. Still, I was clueless. Then Alana said, "She's everybody's cheering squad... everybody's hype man. When you're having a bad day, she's like, 'What do you need?'" JoEve remarked that she "got the role that she wanted" after I encouraged her to audition for a part in the play **In the Heights.**

And then—there she was. My daughter, *Jade,* on the screen. My jaw dropped. My hands started shaking. They were talking about *me.* Jade shared a memory of a time I cleaned her place and cooked for her. "That moment really helped me," she said, her voice filled with emotion. Then she added, "She's a great person, and I'm so proud of her. I thank God for choosing her to be my mother." That's when the tears came. Not the cute kind. The full-blown, ugly cry kind. When they called my name, I stood, legs like jelly, and started toward the stage. The audience was clapping, cheering—but I couldn't hear a thing. My chest tightened, and the room began to spin. I thought, *Lord, I'm about to faint.*

Then I felt a strong, grounding hug. It was Meaders, whispering in my ear, "I'm so proud of you." His calm voice brought me back to the moment, to the space where I was being celebrated. In that instant, I remembered my prayer: "God, help me hear Your voice so clearly that it steadies me in the middle of chaos." Meaders's whisper echoed 1 Kings 19:13: *"And after the fire, a still small voice."* When I finally made it to the stage, my friends from the video were there, along with Jade and our superintendent. I hugged everyone, lingering just a bit longer with Jade, my heart bursting with gratitude.

The days leading up to that moment had been tough. I was struggling with self-doubt—feeling like I wasn't enough as a teacher, a mom, or a wife. But God, in His infinite humor, has a way of sending reminders. That day, surrounded by love and affirmation, I was reminded that *I am enough*. Even now, as I watch the video again (yes, I cried), I feel the same emotions wash over me. And here's the truth: *You are enough, too.* Whether you're a mother, father, daughter, son, teacher, friend—whoever you are—YOU. ARE. ENOUGH.

Sometimes, life surprises us with reminders we didn't know we needed. This one just happened to be wrapped in applause and a standing ovation. Surprise, surprise.

Special shoutout to these special people from Marietta City Schools: Chelsea Bargallo, Joeve Carthers, Natalie Darbey, Dr. Dayton Hibbs, Robert Meaders, Alana McLemore, Zandra Pope, Dr. Grant Rivera, and Yvette Thomas. Thank you for stepping away from your summer to be part of something so unexpected yet incredibly beautiful. Meaders, your timing is always perfect—just when I need a bear hug, you're there, reminding me that I'm never alone. Jade, my sweet girl, having you by my side in such a special moment was more than I could have ever hoped for—it meant everything. And Dr. Rivera, your leadership is filled with so much heart. Thank you for truly seeing me, for recognizing my love for my MMS family, and for making sure others see it too. My heart is full because of each of you.

Because You Made Me Mad

Santana was practically vibrating with excitement—my niece, Lexi's, party was about to start, and she couldn't wait. Her tiny hands gripped the edge of the table as she leaned forward to get a closer look at the cake. It was a masterpiece: pink icing, delicate white flowers, and a shimmering princess crown perched on top. She squinted, trying to make out the words piped in icing. Happy Birthday, Lexi, she thought, though reading wasn't exactly her strong suit at two years old. The cake was mesmerizing, a sugary siren calling to her. She imagined a slice so big it would take her two hands to hold it. Her fantasy was abruptly shattered when I yelled, "Santana, get down!"

Startled, she stumbled back into reality, her daydream evaporating like bubbles in the bath. The tantrum started instantly—a full-body meltdown that could have registered on the Richter scale. Arms flailing, feet kicking, screams echoing. It was the kind of tantrum that would make even seasoned parents cringe. I, however, was a veteran. Without a word, I turned on my heel and walked away, leaving her to thrash on the floor like a fish out of water. Santana paused mid-scream, eyes darting around the room to see if her performance had worked. It hadn't. But then, something shiny caught her eye: a bottle of Mean Green cleaner on the counter. With the sly determination of a toddler on a mission, Santana grabbed the bottle and marched back to the cake. She leaned over, aimed, and sprayed every inch of it with industrial-strength determination, thinking, If I can't have any, nobody else can.

"SANTANA!" I hollered from upstairs. Santana froze, her tiny heart racing. She quickly stashed the cleaner behind the toaster and bolted to her room, leaving the cake a soggy, chemical-laden disaster waiting to be discovered. Hours later, party guests started arriving. Santana, now fully immersed in the chaos of the celebration, bounced with excitement when Lexi and her mama finally walked in. Meanwhile, I buzzed around the house, greeting guests and putting the finishing touches on the party. Santana, her villainous smile returning, seemed confident that I'd forgotten about the cake entirely. But when I headed to the kitchen, her smile disappeared.

I grabbed the cake box and some candles, but as I opened the box to check everything, I was hit with a smell so strong it nearly knocked me over. What in the world?! A quick inspection revealed the horror: the cake was drenched in cleaner. "SANTANA!" I bellowed, my voice echoing through the house. Guests were ushered outside to play games, and Lexi's mama graciously volunteered to supervise. Meanwhile, I was left to deal with the cake and its tiny saboteur. I found Santana hiding under the dining table, her big eyes peeking out, knowing full well she was in trouble. With one swift motion, I grabbed her and gave her a spanking. No explanations, no lectures—just the sound of tiny smacks and her indignant wails.

I sent her to her room, and for a glorious three minutes, there was peace. Then, a little voice called out, "I have to go to the bathroom."

"Come downstairs," I commanded, wary of her solo bathroom antics. Santana sulked down the stairs, dragging her feet like a prisoner walking to the gallows. She slipped into the bathroom and shut the door. Two minutes of silence. I knew better.

I flung the door open, and there it was: my beautiful purse, my lifeline, my everything—violated. Santana had pooped in my purse. I froze, equal parts furious and incredulous. What kind of possessed child— Storming upstairs, I tried to collect myself, but my mama walked in just in time. She scooped Santana up and held her like she was rescuing a war orphan. "Santana," she asked, her voice soft but firm, "Why would you do such a thing?" Santana, with all the confidence of a toddler who knows she's untouchable in Grandma's arms, replied, "Because she made me mad."

Mama whisked her away, sparing her from any further consequences, while I stood there, clutching my violated purse, wondering how life had come to this. Santana may have won that battle, but I'll tell you this—she'll never forget the day she squared off with me and a bottle of Mean Green. Neither will I.

Misunderstandings
(1997-2010)

Jade popped into the kitchen, her little curls bouncing, and asked, "Granma, can I have a peanut jelly sandwich?" Grandma Kathy frowned, adjusting her glasses as she rummaged through the fridge. "Baby, we out of jelly. You want just peanut butter on it?" Jade nodded with all the seriousness a three-year-old could muster. "Yes ma'am, one bread." Grandma Kathy chuckled, slapped some peanut butter on a slice of bread, and handed it to Jade, who grabbed it and dashed off toward the playroom. "Jade, you want some barbecue Vienna's?" Grandma called after her.
From the other room, Jade's voice rang out with excitement, "WITH HOT SAUCE?" Grandma Kathy grinned. "Yeah, come get 'em."

Jade came flying back into the kitchen, her little legs working overtime. As Grandma Kathy set the plate of Vienna sausages on the table, she peered over her glasses. "Jade, where ya sandwich?" Jade, looking thoroughly confused, pointed back toward the playroom. "It's in the playroom," she said innocently. Grandma Kathy threw her hands up. "Don't leave it unattended!" With the sweetest face, Jade replied, "It's not on the tended. It's on the couch." Grandma Kathy burst out laughing, shaking her head at the sheer brilliance of toddler logic. I often look back on moments like these with my girls and marvel at their innocence. Jade was three, Santana just a few months old. Life was simpler then.

Fast forward to today, and I find myself sitting across from them at CiCi's Pizza, ready to have one of our "serious talks." It's one of our rituals—neutral territory with a buffet of distractions in case things get too heavy. "I just heard something disturbing today," I started, trying to ease into the topic. "Do you remember Bill Nye the Science Guy?"

Their faces lit up instantly. They launched into the theme song with the kind of enthusiasm only kids can muster. Jade stood up, flailing her arms and chanting, "BILL, BILL, BILL, BILL!" like it was a sacred anthem. I couldn't help but laugh. "Okay, okay," I said, waving my hands to calm them down. "Let's leave Bill with some dignity. I need to talk to y'all about something serious."

I leaned forward, folding my hands like I was about to deliver a groundbreaking revelation. "If someone challenged your relationship with God, how would you handle it? Would you stand your ground? What would you say?" Jade rolled her eyes at Santana, who responded with her signature sass. "What happened now, Metny?" I sighed, explaining the debate I'd seen between a scientist and a Christian. I softened the edges, changing names to protect their innocence, and relayed how the scientist claimed Christians weren't smart enough to contribute meaningfully to science.

Jade leaned back, her face lighting up with the passion of a preacher at a revival. "Science is fascinating," she began, launching into a well-articulated monologue about the Big Bang Theory. I couldn't follow half of it, but I was captivated nonetheless. She paused, her eyes narrowing as she delivered the punchline: "As much as I love science, I can't see science without God. I don't care how many times you bang two rocks together—it ain't gonna make a human." I stifled a laugh as she went on, her voice steady and wise beyond her years. "Science can't prove or disprove God's existence. You just have to know Him for yourself." Then she turned to Santana with a smirk. "Your turn, big head."

Santana, never one to be rushed, took a deliberate bite of her pizza, wiped her mouth, and sipped her drink like she was about to deliver the State of the Union. Finally, with her face set like a flint, she said, "If someone try to tell me God ain't real, Imma say: 'I am a child of God. Amen, praise the Lord, hallelujah, and if you a bill collector, I rebuke you in the name of Jesus.'"

Jade and I erupted in laughter, tears streaming down our faces. But deep down, I knew Santana was serious. Her bold declaration reminded me of Ecclesiastes 12:13: "Let us hear the conclusion of the whole matter: Fear God, and keep His commandments: for this is the whole duty of man."

Sitting there, I realized my girls had exceeded my expectations. Each, in her own way, had articulated her faith— one with eloquence, the other with unshakable conviction. The seeds I'd sown over the years were blooming right before my eyes. Life is funny that way. We're all at different stages in our walk with God, but what matters is that we're walking. I can't judge someone else's journey; I can only focus on my own and let my love for others speak louder than my words ever could. As I watched my girls giggle and steal bites of each other's pizza, my heart swelled with gratitude. Their faith was their own, and their walks were unique, but one thing was certain— they were walking, and so was I.

The Thorntons

Before I met Kelcey, I was tiptoeing through the wild and unpredictable world of online dating—a journey full of near-disasters, cringe-worthy moments, and more than a few *"what was I thinking?"* dates. It got so bad that I finally dropped to my knees in desperation and prayed, *Lord, block anyone who's going to waste my time with superficial nonsense!* I was *done* with messages like, "What's up, sexy?" or "Hey beautiful, what are you doing tonight?" No depth, no substance, no clue about who I was.

"Lord," I prayed, *"What is wrong with, 'Hello! I hope you have a great day'?"* Surely, someone out there could manage at least that much. And then there he was—**KThornton73.** His first message? "Hello Sunshine! Have a great day!" Little did I know, the man behind that screen was so much more than his description. *"Okay with children"* it said, but Kelcey wasn't just okay—he was extraordinary. This man, who would later become PawPaw, would walk barefoot across the desert to provide for his kids. He had a calming magic; kids—any kids—would curl up in his lap, and even the child with boundless energy would fall asleep like a bear in hibernation.

"Attends church" seemed like an understatement for someone whose life revolves around ministry. He didn't just sit in the pews; he built the church—literally. From fixing walls to running the sound system, protecting the pastor, and ministering to the people, his service was boundless. And then there was his *"best feature—his smile."* When I first saw him, it was like a scene from a rom-com in slow motion. At 6'2", he was a tall glass of chocolate milk—smooth, sweet, and irresistible. When he hugged me for the first time, the world slowed down. He smelled amazing, his hands were warm, and when he smiled, it felt like home. I fit perfectly by his side.

The First Date

On our first date, we went to see **21 and Over**. I had just tortured myself at a fitness boot camp and could barely move, but he never teased me. Instead, he opened every door for me, twirling me around when I ended up on the wrong side, turning my clumsiness into a charming dance. At Waffle House afterward, we fed the jukebox and discovered our mutual love for musical randomness. Maxwell and Carrie Underwood. Aerosmith and Jill Scott. Bon Jovi and Waylon Jennings. It was like our playlists were destined to collide. Sitting there with him, laughing over cheesy grits and jukebox gems, I thought, This guy is just as weird as I am, and I love it.

The Proposal

Kelcey wasn't sure about much in life, having lost his mother at 14. Emotions weren't his thing, and love wasn't something he expressed freely. Yet with me, he was sure. *"Once upon a time, there was a boy who loved a girl, and her laughter was a question he wanted to spend his whole life answering,"* a Nicole Krauss quote, captured how he brought peace to my life. When he proposed, my mind tried to replay every mistake and heartbreak from my past. But my heart knew him. It shut down the fear, replacing it with the sweetness of his touch.

For our wedding, I wrote him a song—a testament to the love we shared. It wasn't just poetry; it was our story in melody: *"The beat of our hearts is the melody, playing over and over our whole life long. When I look into your eyes, and you hold me in your arms, I know that we're living a love song."*

A Lifetime Together

Eleven years, six children, and five grandchildren later, we've gone from Methany and Kelcey to Shooby and PawPaw. We've survived congestive heart failure, high blood pressure, a stroke, shoulder surgery, total knee replacement—you name it. Yet here we are, stronger than ever. Kelcey is my steady anchor, my calm in the storm. When I see him now, I can tell his mood just by the rhythm of his leg swaying. His laugh is deep, lighting up his whole face, and his love for others is shown in actions rather than empty words. He's my one-of-a-kind blessing, changing my life in ways I never thought possible. Doctors once said his heart would never operate at more than 51%, and his prognosis was grim. However, they didn't account for faith, love, and God's miracles. His love saved my life, and maybe, just maybe, mine saved his too.

Looking Ahead

Our love isn't flashy or loud, but it's solid and true. It's the kind of love that turns everyday moments into blessings and every challenge into victories. As I look ahead to our "couple of forevers," I can't help but smile. What started with "Hello Sunshine! Have a great day" became the adventure of a lifetime, filled with laughter, healing, and the kind of love that leaves you breathless.

So, *Lord, thank You for answering my prayer and sending me exactly who I needed—someone who didn't just say the right thing but lived it every single day.*

The Gift

For as long as I can remember, I've had a profound connection to the spiritual realm—a sensitivity that allows me to see things before they happen through visions and dreams. When someone shares their story with me, their words come alive, transforming into vivid scenes that play out in my mind. I don't just hear their words; I experience their emotions, their struggles, and their hopes. This gift has always been with me, but it wasn't until I began seeking God for my true purpose that I fully understood its depth. My soul craves more of Him—not just in the sanctuary, but in every corner of my life. I want to feel God's presence as deeply in my home, at work, in my car, and during quiet moments of personal prayer and worship as I do in powerful church services. I long for His Spirit to permeate every space I inhabit, filling it with His peace, love, and glory.

During a ministerial training class, my pastor asked me what I believed my spiritual gift was. Without hesitation, I responded, "Prophetic and healing." At that moment, I couldn't claim to be fully operating in those gifts, but I was determined to dive deeper, to glean every bit of wisdom and understanding I could. I've always been peculiar, seeing the world through a lens that others often don't understand. Over time, I've come to embrace this difference, recognizing it as part of God's divine design for my life. One of my greatest gifts is faith—the kind that clings to God's Word as truth the moment it's spoken. This faith isn't just for me; it's for those who need hope, healing, and a reminder that God is still working.

Another gift God entrusted to me is forgiveness. It's a trait that's been passed down like an heirloom—from my grandmother to my mother, and from my mother to me. Forgiving those who trespass against us isn't just an act of grace; it's an essential part of ministering to God's people. Yet, I had to learn to walk out my own purpose with this gift, leaning on God for the strength to forgive and intercede.

But my hunger for God goes beyond knowing my gifts. I want to experience Him in every aspect of my life. I refuse to settle for routine encounters or moments of distant reverence. Every time I enter His throne room, I want to feel His tangible glory. I want to bring others with me into His presence, leading them into worship as I worship, showing them how to encounter Him for themselves. When God moves in a service, I feel it with an intensity that goes beyond my own emotions. I can sense the pain, anguish, and hurt of others as though they're my own. Their unspoken cries stir something deep within me, driving me to intercede on their behalf. I lay hands on the sick, believing God for their healing, and I've seen His miraculous power at work time and time again.

I am a worshipper at my core. When I sing, it's not just melody; it's an offering, a pathway into His presence. Worship is the language of my soul. It is how I pour out my heart to Him and how I lead others into sacred communion with the Creator. As I go deeper into worship, I bring others with me, guiding them into that sacred space where God's Spirit moves freely. Worship isn't just something I do; it's who I am. I want this same intimacy with God in every moment of my life. Whether I'm cooking dinner, driving to work, or sitting quietly in my living room, I want to feel His presence just as powerfully as when I'm singing my heart out in a church service. I want my life to be an altar, my heart a sanctuary where His Spirit dwells continually.

I am a chosen vessel, called to intercede, to worship, to prophesy, and to heal. My heart beats for His will, and my life's purpose is to see it fulfilled—not just in my life but in the lives of everyone I encounter. I long for them to feel the fullness of His love, the power of His presence, and the depth of His grace. This is the gift He has given me, and with every fiber of my being, I will use it to glorify Him.

The Sanctuary

After a rough week, I know I need time with God. My soul craves it, and there's only one place I want to be: the sanctuary. As I pull into the parking lot, I can't help but smile. There's no one else here yet—it's just me and the stillness of His presence. This is my favorite time, a moment when I can let everything go without pretense. I unlock the doors and step inside, leaving the lights off. The sunlight streams through the windows, creating a soft, sacred glow. It's just enough to see my way but dim enough to feel intimate and peaceful. As I walk toward the altar, it's as if my burdens are falling off with every step. The weight of my circumstances grows faint, replaced by the sweet anticipation of being with God.

When I reach the altar, I collapse to my knees, tears already streaming down my face. I cry out to Him, pouring everything I've been holding inside. The silence of the sanctuary doesn't bother me; in fact, it feels like God is listening, waiting patiently for me to give Him all of it. I start to sing, letting my voice rise to awaken His presence, inviting Him to fill the room. My prayers follow, pouring out in waves. I pray for my pastor and his family, for the congregation, for the upcoming service. I ask God to saturate this place with His glory, to make it a refuge where His people will leave refreshed, strengthened, and renewed. I pray for anything not of Him to be removed—every obstacle, every distraction—so that when the people come, they will find nothing but love, peace, and His overwhelming presence.

This sanctuary is more than just a building to me. It's my fortress, my hiding place, my secret meeting spot with God. Before my wedding, I came here. I laid on this very floor, pouring out my nervous jitters and doubts, and this place wrapped me up in God's peace. It became my steady ground when everything felt like it was spinning. Before every service, it's the sanctuary that covers me, fills me with His glory, and prepares me to minister to hundreds of people. It's the place where my heart aligns with His will, where I remember that I'm not doing this alone.

I smile as I think about what this place becomes when the congregation arrives. The music begins to play, and your walls reverberate with the sounds of worship. Voices rise in unison, creating a melody so powerful it feels like heaven is leaning in to listen. Tears of joy and repentance soak the carpet as hearts are healed and chains are broken. The preached word moves through your halls like a two-edged sword, cutting through doubt and despair, leaving truth and hope in its place. Testimonies of God's goodness spill into the air, echoing from person to person. Within these walls, the broken are mended, the weary are strengthened, and the lost are found.

You are more than a building. You are a hospital for the sin-sick, a training ground for those called to minister beyond these walls. In your openness, unity springs forth. Brotherhood is birthed. The love of God radiates from your very foundation, touching all who enter. Some people say, "I can worship at home," and they're right—but my home is a chaotic symphony of barking dogs, ringing phones, blaring TVs, and the occasional intrusive cat. My neighbors shout at each other with words that cut, and cars rumble across gravel driveways, leaving me struggling to find a moment of peace. I could try to worship in a closet, but even there, the distractions find me.

However, when I step into the sanctuary, all of that fades away. Here, there are no distractions—only the presence of God waiting for me. It's as though He stands in the corridors, ready to meet me like lovers drawn together for an embrace. My mind clears. My heart fills. My spirit breathes. This is where I find Him, where I hear His whispers over the noise of life. This sanctuary makes it possible for me to lay everything at His feet, to worship freely, and to leave filled with His peace. It's my place of refuge, my holy ground. Before the service, before the people, before the noise, it's just me, God, and the sanctuary. And in those moments, I am reminded that His presence is everything I need.

The Healing
September 2016

      Just sitting down to write this makes my heart race. As I type, I've carefully chosen a cheerful font, hoping it might lighten the weight of my emotions.

Nineteen years ago, I gave birth to a son. He never opened his eyes. He never took a breath. He never cried or laughed. His name was Ryan Hakeem, which means "little king." He was a gift—one I now wonder if I cherished enough at the time. But I can't dwell on that. Why would I?

Eighteen years ago, I gave birth to a daughter. She entered this world with a stubborn, piercing cry that softened the moment she was placed in my arms. She was a tiny replica of her father, perfect in every way. Her name is Santana Brooke Evans Butler. Her name, when written out, was longer than her little body. She, too, was a gift.

Nineteen years ago, I left the hospital empty. My arms were empty. My heart was empty. The pain I endured bore no reward, only scars that no one could see but me. And then came the questions—silent accusations in the glances of strangers and whispers that didn't need to be spoken. *Where's your baby?*

Eighteen years ago, I left the hospital with a princess the nurses affectionately called "Peanut." She weighed 5 pounds, 15 ounces—a tiny miracle. As I held her, love overwhelmed me again, fresh and pure. She was my peace, my reminder that joy could still bloom after heartbreak.

Their birthdays are only two days apart, a bittersweet overlap. Each year, I celebrate Santana's life while quietly mourning Ryan's. The loss of one has haunted the joy of the other, and no matter how hard I try, I can't shake the sadness that comes with it. I smile through the birthday celebrations, but inside, my heart aches. I've often wondered, Will I ever be normal again? Two years ago, I woke up days before their birthdays with a plan: stay busy, stay focused. I cleaned from sunrise to sunset for two days straight, then celebrated for seven more. I had found my cure—distraction. If I kept myself busy enough, maybe I could escape the hurt. And for a while, it worked. I felt normal.

This year, the birthdays came again. My schedule was packed. After school on Friday, I drove to Alabama to sing, sharing laughs and life updates with a good friend on the ride there. We didn't mention Ryan. I sang my heart out in Alabama, then headed back to Georgia for Santana's birthday celebration. The drive back was a solo concert, me belting out every song that came on the radio, oblivious to the amused stares of drivers who passed me. I arrived home feeling accomplished, nostalgic, and—finally—normal. But grief doesn't follow a schedule.

I woke up Sunday morning, and it hit me like a ton of bricks. I couldn't breathe. Grief sat heavy on my chest, suffocating my joy. I had to minister to God's people that day, but how could I? Who would I encourage when I felt so broken? And who could encourage me? The next five days felt unbearable. Well-meaning words from friends and loved ones only made things worse. No one could pull me out of the dark, and I realized this was something I had to face with God alone. I know God is powerful. I know He loves me. He can do anything. He was waiting for me to surrender my sadness to Him, to let Him wrap me in His peace like a warm blanket on a cold, dark night. And so I prayed: *"God, I'm sad. I don't want to be sad anymore. Please help me. Turn my mourning into dancing like You promised. Turn my sorrow into joy. Give me beauty for these ashes. I can't go on like this."*

And He answered.

Now, when I look at Santana, I thank God she's here. I thank Him for entrusting me with such a beautiful gift. And when I think of Ryan, I no longer dwell on the pain. Instead, I remember that he's with the King of Kings, watching over me and his sisters. My little king is in the arms of the ultimate King, and one day, I'll see him again. Ryan was my only son, a gift that God chose to call back home. Why he had to go so soon, I'll never understand—but I can't dwell on that. Why would I? God, in His grace, has given me so much to hold onto, including a princess who reminds me every day that joy is still possible. So, I carry both—the sorrow and the joy—knowing that God has been with me through it all, turning my ashes into something beautiful.

Outside Looking In
(2024)

As I reflect on my writing journey, I notice a pattern emerging—a way of using words to peer into my life as if I were an outsider looking in. Writing memoirs has become my way of processing the lessons from my past, a tool for learning and healing. Strangely, many of my recent pieces have been steeped in grief, loss, and memories of childhood. This exploration of darker themes revealed a side of myself I hadn't fully acknowledged. I've always prided myself on being able to laugh through life's challenges, but writing has forced me to confront emotions that laughter cannot mask. There's a common thread woven through my work, one that's hard to ignore: death. It's not an easy subject to write about, nor an easy truth to face. But as a nonfiction writer, I hope to offer readers a glimpse into life's highs and lows—the joy and the pain. While I aspire to focus more on the joys, I've realized that confronting the pain is just as important. Writing is my battleground, my way of combating life's complexities with a pen and a notebook.

A Healing Journey

Through my stories, I've confronted memories that have shaped me—some beautiful, others haunting. In pieces like "The Healing" and "You'll See," I've revisited moments of heartbreak, like the loss of my son Ryan and the bittersweet reality of celebrating my daughter Santana's life each year. Their birthdays, just two days apart, carry an emotional weight that I can't escape. Ryan's absence lingers in Santana's celebrations, and every smile hides a quiet ache. Grief has become a companion I never asked for. At times, it feels like a heavy raincoat I can't take off, even when the storm has passed. But writing about these moments has allowed me to glimpse healing in the midst of the sorrow. Each word is a step forward, a small act of reclaiming joy while honoring the pain.

Facing the Dragon

One revelation struck me as I re-read my writing: I have an issue with sadness. Watching the movie **Inside Out** and **Inside Out 2** brought this to light. I resonated with *Joy*'s frustration toward *Sadness*, wanting to brush her aside and move on. But life doesn't work like that. Just as *Joy* learned to embrace *Sadness*'s role, I've begun to see that grief and healing coexist. My past has taught me that healing isn't about erasing pain; it's about finding peace within it. But *Sadness* hasn't been my only companion. *Anxiety, Embarrassment, and Envy* have also played their roles in shaping my journey—each bringing its own challenges, lessons, and eventual growth.

Anxiety is the loudest of the bunch, constantly chattering in the back of my mind. She shows up uninvited, pacing back and forth, wringing her hands, and shouting, "What if?!" What if they think you're not good enough? What if you fail? What if the storm doesn't pass this time? She's the one who makes surprises unbearable, turning the unknown into a monster lurking around every corner. From the childhood memory of being unprepared for Mommee's funeral to the adult fear of being blindsided by life's twists, *Anxiety* has been relentless. Yet, in her persistence, she has taught me to prepare, to pray, and to trust God's control when I can't see the full picture.

Embarrassment is quieter, but he lingers longer. He likes to replay my most vulnerable moments like a highlight reel I can't escape. He reminds me of the time I screamed uncontrollably at Mommee's funeral, my young voice piercing the somber quiet. He replays my reaction to the "Be Somebody" award, when I didn't recognize myself in the glowing descriptions of others, and I almost fainted as I approached the stage.

Embarrassment whispers, "See? You're too much. You're not enough." But through those moments, I've learned that vulnerability isn't weakness—it's a bridge to connection. *Embarrassment* has forced me to confront the parts of myself I'd rather hide, showing me that authenticity often shines brightest through imperfections.

And then there's *Envy*, sly and subtle, creeping in when I least expect her. She doesn't throw tantrums like *Anxiety* or linger like *Embarrassment*; instead, she sows quiet discontent. She's the voice that wonders why others seem to glide through life with ease while I carry the weight of grief, health challenges, and self-doubt. She whispered when I saw others with healthy children after losing Ryan. She reappeared when I struggled to celebrate others' successes during moments when I felt unseen. But *Envy*, for all her cunning, has been a surprising teacher. She's revealed the desires I hold deep in my heart—desires for peace, joy, and purpose. And by facing her, I've learned to channel those feelings into gratitude for my own blessings and a deeper compassion for others.

Together, *Anxiety, Embarrassment, Envy, and Sadness* form a peculiar chorus, each singing their own part in my life's song. At times, their voices have been overwhelming, drowning out the melodies of *Joy*, Peace, and Faith. But I'm learning to conduct this symphony, giving each voice its moment while ensuring they don't dominate the score. Life isn't about silencing these emotions but understanding their roles. *Sadness* reminds me to honor what I've lost. *Anxiety* pushes me to lean into God's promises. *Embarrassment* teaches me humility and courage. *Envy* challenges me to grow in gratitude. Together, they've helped me see that healing isn't a destination but a journey—a process of embracing every part of who I am.

As I continue writing, I hope to give these characters their due acknowledgment, not as villains, but as vital parts of my story. They've helped me face the dragons of grief, insecurity, and longing. And as I walk this path of healing, I'm reminded again of Psalm 27:14: "Wait on the Lord. Be of good courage, and He shall strengthen your heart." Even when the dragons roar, I trust God's still, small voice saying, "Methany... you'll see." And I believe Him.

Encouragement in Reflection

In one of my darkest moments, I prayed for God to turn my mourning into dancing, my sorrow into joy. He answered—not by erasing the grief, but by giving me the strength to carry it differently. I've learned to wait on Him, trusting in His timing even when it feels unbearable, remembering Psalm 27:14. Through writing, I've discovered a profound truth: healing is a process, not a destination. Every story I write, every tear I shed, is part of that process. It's not about forgetting the pain, but about embracing the lessons it brings. And in those lessons, I find hope. To anyone reading this, let me encourage you: it's okay to grieve, to feel the weight of sadness, to sit in the discomfort of the unknown. But don't stay there. Keep moving forward, one step at a time. Healing awaits—not in denying the storm, but in learning to dance in the rain.

Hidden Eclipse
(August 2017)

      The scriptures spoke of the full blood moon, and I couldn't wait to witness the splendor of God's creation. All day Sunday, I eagerly anticipated this lunar eclipse, imagining the brilliance of the heavens displaying God's handiwork. As night fell, the darkness in our neighborhood set the stage perfectly—there were no streetlights, only the quiet hum of nature and the silhouette of the big tree in our front yard. That tree, our makeshift garage, served as home to ants, mosquitoes, and all things itchy. Its branches were notorious for dropping uninvited "guests" onto innocent bystanders. Armed with flashlights from our phones, Santana and I ventured into the night, navigating carefully to avoid stepping on anything that might crawl or scurry. "They been talking about this all week at school," Santana announced confidently, "and Imma get me a picture of this 'seclipse.'" Her mispronunciation made me chuckle, but I couldn't resist correcting her. "It's eclipse, Santana." She waved me off with a smile, determined to use her own words, as always.

      We made our way to the opening of the neighborhood, where a short brick wall beckoned us like a star-gazer's bench. We sat down, craning our necks toward the sky, hearts full of anticipation. For me, this wasn't just a celestial event—it was a moment rich with spiritual significance. The scriptures in Joel spoke of a "full blood moon," a prophecy fulfilled. The air was thick with expectation. But then came the clouds. A thick, unyielding blanket of them rolled across the sky, hiding the moon from view. Santana groaned in frustration, holding up her iPhone to snap what turned out to be a picture of—well... clouds. Beautiful, fluffy, moon-obscuring clouds. "This is so unfair," she huffed, staring at her screen. "I wanted to see it for real!" Her disappointment was palpable, but I saw an opportunity for something deeper.

I looked up at the obscured sky, smiled, and turned to her. "Santana, just because we can't see the moon doesn't mean it's not there," I said gently. "It's still up there, shining and doing exactly what it was created to do. The clouds are just in the way." She looked at me skeptically, her frustration still simmering. So, I pressed on. "This is a lot like our faith in God. We can't always see Him, and sometimes, life throws up clouds that block our view. But does that mean He's not there? No. He's always present, working behind the scenes, just like the moon is lighting the night somewhere else, even if we can't see it right now."

She was quiet for a moment, her face thoughtful. "So, somebody else gets to see the 'seclipse' because they need it more than us?" she asked. Her honesty tugged at my heart. "Exactly," I said with a smile. "Someone else might need to see this to be reminded that God is real, that He's always there. And maybe what we needed tonight wasn't to see the eclipse but to remember that our faith doesn't depend on what we can see." Santana tilted her head, a small smile tugging at her lips. "Still wish I could've gotten my picture, though."

We both laughed, and in that moment, I felt a peace that the clouds couldn't dim. The moon, hidden but present, reminded me that faith isn't about what's visible—it's about trust, even in the unseen. Somewhere, someone was watching that glorious blood moon and being reminded of God's majesty, and right here, beneath a cloud-covered sky, I was reminded of His presence in my life.

Blending the Right Way
(2023)

The 1998 movie Stepmom has always been a tearjerker for me. Watching Julia Roberts' character, Isabel, and Susan Sarandon's Jackie navigate the complexities of blended family life struck a chord. I never wanted to be anyone's stepmom—I was determined to avoid the title altogether. If my children ever had to deal with a stepmother, I promised myself I'd be like Jackie: respectful, yet fiercely guarded. Watching the movie, I initially disliked both characters for the chaos they brought into their children's lives. But by the end, when they became a unified team with the shared goal of their children's happiness, I was sobbing uncontrollably. If the opportunity ever arose in my life, I vowed to treat my spouse's children as I would want mine to be treated.

That was then.

In our home, we don't use the words stepmom, stepdad, or stepchildren. We are simply The Thorntons. Our family includes Kelcey, Methany, Samantha, Monsanto, Santino, April, Ashley, Jade, Santana, Tyanna, Isaiah, and Isaac. Yes, six children, but many more hearts. We're what we proudly call a "parental unit." We've chosen to define our family not by labels but by love and commitment. Was it always like this? Of course not. Blending families is messy, complex, and often misunderstood, but when done with intentionality, it becomes something beautiful.

According to the U.S. Census Bureau, 1,300 new stepfamilies are formed every day. Judith Wallerstein once reported that children of divorce tend to thrive when parents, regardless of remarriage, resume parenting roles, set aside differences, and maintain strong relationships with their children. Sadly, only a few children experience this level of cooperation. I am determined that my family will be the exception, not the rule.

I remember meeting my bonus babies for the first time. Nervous and excited, I wanted to make a good impression. I knew they adored their dad, and I was just hoping to fit into their world without forcing it. What I didn't expect was meeting their mom, Samantha, at the same time. I thought to myself, "She's cute." That's all I could muster! But I focused on the kids, answering their questions honestly and showing them who I truly was. It was easy to love them—especially Tya, who was as sassy and strong-willed as my own Santana. Watching those two interact was like witnessing a mirror duel of quick wit and attitude.

Samantha and I didn't have a perfect start. We fumbled through misunderstandings and awkward moments, learning how to communicate along the way. Over time, our relationship transformed. Instead of being adversaries, we became advocates for one another, co-parents, and, eventually, friends. I'll never forget the day Samantha asked me to marry Kelcey—not just for him, but on behalf of her and the kids. I laughed, I cried, and politely stated that I don't think that's how it works.

Our journey has taught me valuable lessons about love, inclusion, and humility. Samantha has become a sister to me, and her children are my children. Her grace taught me how to include my daughter's other mom, April, in everything. I make sure she knows how much I appreciate her role in Santana's life. This has encouraged Kelcey and Jade's dad, Monsanto, to work alongside Kelcey to ensure Jade feels supported by both of her fathers. I hold Kelcey accountable for being emotionally and financially present for all of his children, ensuring phone calls, birthday dinners, and extra hugs happen without fail.

Blending families isn't about pretending everyone gets along perfectly all the time—it's about showing up. It's about creating a safe space for the children to know they don't have to choose sides. They can love everyone equally without fear of guilt or betrayal. Society often portrays stepfamilies as chaotic, filled with jealousy and rivalry. But we have the power to rewrite that narrative. I challenge all blended families to take a step back and focus on what truly matters: the happiness and well-being of the children. Build bridges instead of walls. Find common ground and let love lead.

I'll never forget receiving a text from Samantha during a particularly tough time. She wrote:

"Bio, adoptive, foster, step... It's not the word before the parent that defines, but rather the love and dedication in the parent's heart. I'm thankful for you."

Her words still bring tears to my eyes and remind me that this isn't just about blending families—it's about creating a legacy of love. Together, we've shown our children that family isn't defined by blood but by the bonds we choose to nurture. Blended families, I encourage you: Be the exception. Be the light. Show the world that unity is possible, and that the love shared between parents—biological and bonus—can make all the difference. As Jackie said in Stepmom: *"The truth is, she doesn't have to choose. She can have us both, love us both. And she'll become a better person because of me and because of you."* Our kids are stronger because they are surrounded by a team of parents who love, support, and sacrifice for them daily. Blending families the right way is hard work, but the joy of seeing our children flourish is worth every effort. Let's create a path for other families to follow, one filled with love, patience, and understanding. After all, we're not just blended—we're blessed.

Piece of My Heart
(2013)

    The bittersweet news came: Elijah, my nephew who is Jade's twin cousin, was heading off to boot camp to join the Marines, following in the footsteps of my nephew Kelsey (Marines) and my niece Kayla (Air Force). My respect for the military had always run deep, but now it felt personal—like pieces of my heart were being pulled out and sent to God only knew where.

    Elijah, my jokester, wasn't one to take life too seriously. I remembered someone's advice to him before he left: "Get serious! They'll try to beat that laughter out of you." The thought made my head ache. I vowed to pray for Elijah every single day while he was away, knowing Marine training was as brutal as it was transformative. The summer of 2013 became a season of prayer—a burden I couldn't ignore, even if I tried.

    Months passed, and the stories rolled in—brief phone calls home, letters filled with exhaustion, and tales of resilience. I saw Kelsey return home before being stationed in Japan, his demeanor completely changed. The boy I had known had given way to the Marine. Standing in my sister's living room one evening, we watched the news report about the missing Malaysian plane. Kelsey, my nephew, disappeared right before my eyes, replaced by a Marine. The weight of his transformation made my heart ache for Elijah, for Kayla, for all of them. Would they emerge with their hearts intact? Would they still laugh, cry, and love the way they used to? I prayed not only for their safety but for the preservation of the sweet souls they were before they left.

June 2014 arrived faster than I was ready for. The day of Elijah's graduation came, and we packed into a convoy to see him. My heart raced as we took our seats on the bleachers. I prayed silently, thanking God for keeping Elijah safe through training. The ceremony was a whirlwind of pride, patriotism, and tears—fathers standing tall, mothers wiping their cheeks, grandparents beaming with joy. It was beautiful and overwhelming. As the ceremony ended, we stepped down to greet our Marine. I held back, watching as Elijah embraced his mom, dad, and siblings. My heart felt like it would burst. Finally, he approached me, his eyes glistening with tears. When he hugged me, it was as if time stopped. "You had a rough time, huh?" I asked, trying to hold back my own tears. He nodded, his voice breaking as he said, "I prayed for y'all every day."

His words unraveled me. My mind flooded with memories: his baby days under a heat lamp for jaundice, his sheep-like little voice, the blonde afro he sported as a toddler, his endless corny jokes, his love for cornbread, and the way he adored my daughter with an unbreakable bond. Elijah had endured the taunts, the grueling drills, and the loneliness of boot camp, and yet his thoughts were of us. He prayed for us. Even then, he was grasping the essence of sacrifice, preparing himself to protect and provide for his family. Later that night, I helped him with his new watch. As I adjusted the strap, I realized life would never be the same. He was home for now, but soon he'd leave again. There was still the question of where he would be stationed, but my heart felt peace. God had been faithful, and I trusted Him to keep Elijah safe.

Then, God answered another prayer. Kelsey was stationed first—Okinawa, Japan. Next, Kayla—Okinawa, Japan. And then Elijah—yes, Okinawa, Japan. It felt like divine alignment, a gift that they would have each other. Elijah even gave Kayla away at her wedding, a moment that brought our family closer despite the distance. Though parts of my heart now reside halfway across the world, technology allows us to speak weekly, and God fills in the gaps where I cannot be. He is their protector, their provider, their ever-present help.

To veterans and active military personnel and their families, I say thank you. Thank you for your sacrifice, your strength, and your unwavering commitment to our country. You carry burdens most of us can't imagine, and you do it with courage and grace. To families like ours, whose hearts stretch across time zones and battlefields, know that God is there, holding us together in ways only He can. So tonight, when you pray, please remember the brave men and women who serve and the families who stand behind them. We may not always see the battles they fight or the sacrifices they make, but their love and dedication ensure our freedom. And to Elijah, Kelsey, Kayla, and now Bubba, thank you for being a part of that legacy. You are my heroes, and you'll always hold a piece of my heart.

Wonder Woman
(1982)

When I was about seven, Wonder Woman wasn't just a character on TV—she was my alter ego. Every episode of the original series transfixed me, and during my playtime, I transformed into her. One day, after an especially action-packed episode, I dashed outside, ready to save the world. My destination? My favorite tree, a secret hideaway where Methany disappeared, and Wonder Woman emerged. Spinning in circles, I transformed. The world blurred around me, and suddenly, I wasn't a little girl anymore. I was her, the iconic Amazon warrior. I fought invisible villains relentlessly, wrapping them in my trusty (but invisible) Lasso of Truth. They spilled secrets about hidden candy stashes, stolen jewels, and daring bank heists. For over two hours, I battled tirelessly, saving the world one truth at a time. No one could rival me—I was the superhero of the neighborhood.

But then came a voice that broke through my heroic haze. "Methany!" Mama was calling me. Except...she wasn't calling for Wonder Woman. She was calling for the other me. I couldn't risk answering. What if the villains overheard? My cover would be blown! I pressed on, ignoring the calls.

Finally, after my world-saving energy depleted, I spun back into Methany and dashed into the house for water. I flung open the door and ran right into Mama. Let's just say the next few minutes weren't my proudest. As she delivered one of the most memorable spankings of my life, I tried to explain my silence. "Mama, I couldn't answer! The bad guys would know who Wonder Woman really is!" Mama wasn't having it. With every swat, I couldn't stop thinking how badly I needed Wonder Woman's indestructible Bracelets of Victory. Alas, even superheroes have weaknesses. Superman has kryptonite. My Achilles' heel? Mama.

Years later, I told this story to my friend and fellow teacher, Natalie. We laughed until tears ran down our faces, and then the memory faded into the chaos of school life. I thought nothing more of it—until one particularly challenging day of teaching during the pandemic. Natalie stopped by my classroom with a small, wrapped gift. Inside was a Wonder Woman bangle. "I thought you might need this," she said, her smile soft and knowing. She remembered that story and wanted to remind me of my inner superhero. I cried. Of course, I cried. That simple act of kindness meant more than words could say, especially during a time when the weight of teaching virtually and navigating an empty classroom felt unbearable. The bangle became my modern-day Bracelets of Victory, a reminder that even when the world feels heavy, I am strong enough to carry it.

Now, I wear that Wonder Woman bangle on hard days—days when I know I'll need superhuman strength to get through. Other times, I put it on at the end of the day as I reflect on the battles I faced. I think about the moments when I chose kindness over anger, grace over frustration, or self-control when I wanted to scream. And in the moments I didn't feel like a superhero—when I stumbled, struggled, or needed forgiveness—I realized something profound. Being Wonder Woman isn't about never faltering; it's about not giving up when you do. Wonder Woman taught me that true strength is in persistence, in showing up, and in the willingness to try again. To all my fellow superheroes out there, fighting your invisible villains and spinning through life's challenges: Don't give up. Whether you're saving the day on your job, at home, or just making it through another tough moment—you are stronger than you think.

So, go ahead. Spin into your superhero self. The world needs you.

The Amazing Michael Jackson
(1982)
Age seven was a wild year for me! (Insert laugh here.)

When I was in second grade, I was one of two Black students in my grade and the only one in my class. It didn't bother me much, though, because I had a secret weapon: my special gift. I could write in cursive. Not just any cursive—fancy, elegant, Michael Jackson-worthy cursive. One day, I came up with an absolutely brilliant plan. It wasn't just a plan; it was a scheme. A masterpiece.

That morning, I woke up with a purpose. I rolled the cuffs of my jeans twice, threw on a crisp white t-shirt under a plaid blazer, slipped on my white socks and penny loafers, and headed to school looking sharp. My outfit screamed "I'm related to greatness," and that's exactly what I needed for my plan to work. During class, I casually mentioned to one of my classmates that Michael Jackson was my uncle. Naturally, the kid was skeptical, so I sweetened the deal. "For just two dollars," I whispered, "I can get you his autograph." Their eyes widened. By the end of the day, word had spread, and I had a line of classmates eager to pay me for a piece of music history. My heart raced like I was dancing to "Beat It" as I quietly pocketed my first few dollars.

That afternoon, I went home and got to work. Sitting in my room, I meticulously forged 15 little slips of paper with my uncle Michael's signature. Each one was a masterpiece, written with the flair of someone who didn't just learn cursive. My hands trembled with excitement. I was unstoppable.

The next day, I arrived at school, ready to make my rounds. With every slip of paper I handed out, the pride on my classmates' faces grew. They weren't just regular kids anymore; they were part of an elite club that had a direct connection to the King of Pop. By mid-morning, I had collected a whopping $22—more money than I'd ever seen in my life.

Enough, I thought, to hit up the book fair and save for the red Thriller jacket with all the zippers. I was on top of the world, but then, it all came crashing down.

      My teacher called me to her desk. "Methany," she said, her voice calm but full of suspicion, "is Michael Jackson your uncle?" I froze. But only for a second. "Uhhh… yes," I said, lifting my chin with confidence. She raised an eyebrow and hit me with an "ummmm, ok," before waving me back to my seat. I breathed a sigh of relief. Close call, I thought. That relief was short-lived. When I got home, Mama was waiting for me in the living room, her arms crossed. "Methany," she started, "where's the money you took from those kids at school?" I considered lying but quickly realized that would be a mistake. Mama had a way of sniffing out the truth. I handed over the money, my dreams of the books from the book fair and my new Thriller jacket slipping through my fingers.

She laughed—a deep, hearty laugh that shook the room. "Girl, stop lying to them kids at that school. You know better," she said. I stood there, fuming. If she thought it was so funny, why didn't she give me my money back? I was furious! Well, she didn't. She kept the money, and I didn't see a single dime of it. My grand entrepreneurial dreams were over before they even began. But did I tell the kids Michael Jackson wasn't my uncle? Absolutely not. I doubled down, letting them think I spent their money on candy. To this day, I imagine they hum *Smooth Criminal* whenever they think of me. Looking back, I laugh at the absurdity of it all. It's one of those childhood stories that reminds me how creative, audacious, and maybe a little mischievous I was. While I never got the Thriller jacket, I did learn a valuable lesson: don't underestimate a seven-year-old with a vivid imagination, a talent for cursive, and a dream.

Ear Infection to Eulogy

The title of this chapter may provoke confusion, even disbelief, but it accurately captures one of the most unimaginable and painful periods of my life. It's a story of love, grief, and ultimately, faith.

I met Savannah Butler in 1995. She was just 10 years old—sassy, full of life, and impossible not to adore. I was dating her brother at the time, but she quickly became my shadow. She and my daughter Jade shared the same middle name, pigeon-toed feet, and a mutual love for food. Savannah was easy to love, her laughter infectious, her presence magnetic. Over the years, she became more than a sister-in-law—she was my family, a part of me. She was also the best aunt to my girls. Her babies were mine, and mine were hers. No matter the twists and turns in my relationship with her brother, Savannah remained steadfast—a constant in my life and in the lives of my children.

On Monday, March 21, 2022, my world shifted. Santana called me hysterical and inconsolable. Her screaming was so intense I couldn't understand her words. I was in the middle of a lesson, teaching my students how to manage their emotions, and had to hang up the phone because I couldn't calm her down. I called back, and this time her boss answered. With a shaky voice, she told me that Savannah was in the hospital and unresponsive. I froze. A million thoughts raced through my mind, but one thing was clear: I had to leave immediately. I radioed for someone to cover my classroom and began packing my things. I didn't even realize I was in a state of panic until the school resource officer and several administrators appeared at my door.

I apologized and explained the situation, then sped home to pick up Santana. Together, we rushed to the hospital in Chattanooga, only to be met with the devastating news: Savannah had been declared brain dead. Four days earlier, she had gone to the hospital for an ear infection. An ear infection. They treated her with steroids and for COVID-19, despite a negative test result. The infection traveled to the meninges of her brain, developing into meningitis by Sunday night. By the time we arrived, machines were the only things keeping her body alive.

How could this happen? How could an ear infection lead to this? The questions were endless, the answers nonexistent.

Fast forward to Saturday afternoon, I was tasked with eulogizing my sweet, borrowed sister. I stood before a room of mourners, still grappling with the shock and pain of it all. How do you find the words to comfort others when you're drowning in your own grief? How do you celebrate a life cut short in such a senseless way? As I wrestled with these questions, God ministered to me. He reminded me of His strength, His love, His sovereignty. He showed me that it was okay not to be strong. That His strength is made perfect in our weakness. That we didn't have to understand to trust Him. The day after the memorial, I sat alone with my grief. I turned to Facebook and wrote:

"I love words...their pronunciation; their meaning. Even making up definitions for imaginary words gives me so much pleasure. This week, as much as I love words, I had absolutely none to explain how I felt. No words to make me understand how this all happened. No words to express how I feel about losing someone that means so much to me. No words to express the shock and numbness that has replaced the words and the feelings that usually come so easily. I do know this...GOD IS FAITHFUL, and HE will bless and keep us and comfort us as we navigate through this new chapter!"

But it wasn't just any chapter. It was the hardest chapter I'd ever had to live. I threw myself into work, hoping the busyness would dull the pain. One day, I sat in my classroom and opened a gift from friends and the cheer squad. The card inside read, "Your sister *was* a beautiful soul." One word wrecked me: *was*. The finality of it hit like a freight train. I sobbed, angry and broken. How was I supposed to teach my students to manage their emotions when I couldn't manage my own? How was I supposed to continue pursuing my doctorate while my nieces and nephew mourned their mother? How was I supposed to live my life normally when my sister had died because someone chose not to listen to her?

As I write this, it's been a year since Savannah did her Hero Walk, donating her organs and saving lives. Even in death, she gave. But living without her has been one of the toughest battles I've faced. Some days, I function well. Others, I feel like I've failed. But grief isn't linear. It sneaks up in unexpected moments—a smell, a sound, a memory. This week, I realized why I felt so off. It's been a year since we lost her. A year since the world dimmed just a little. But even in the sorrow, I hold onto hope. Savannah's life mattered. Her legacy of love, kindness, and sacrifice lives on. To anyone mourning a loved one, take it one day at a time. Some days, all you'll manage is breathing—and that's okay. Trust that God is with you in your grief, offering strength when you have none.

In memory of Savannah Jade Butler
November 29, 1986 - March 21, 2022
Forever loved. Forever missed. Forever cherished.

Grief: The Uninvited Guest

February 1, 2023

I found myself in a meeting, trying to explain how tricky grief can be. One day, you're numb, brushing it off with a casual c'est la vie. The next, grief feels so heavy and suffocating that it literally takes your breath away. Funny thing is, I was completely fine when I walked into that room. But as soon as I began to speak about grief, that heifer showed up—bold and uninvited. There I was, shaking and angry at the sheer audacity of grief to interrupt my life whenever she feels like it. She's disrespectful like that! Tricky and relentless. Ugly in her timing but beautiful in her purpose. She's cold and harsh, yet somehow warm and tender. Grief has this uncanny way of turning memories into emotions that hit like a tidal wave, dragging physical symptoms along for the ride.

Here's what I've learned, though: You can't ignore her. You have to confront her. Grief doesn't knock politely at the door; she barges in. The only way to deal with her is to acknowledge her presence and surrender to whatever lesson she's trying to teach. I'd love to tell you it gets easier, but truthfully, I'm not there yet.

A Day Later

Yesterday, I journaled about grief. I referred to her as a woman, and let me tell you, I wasn't kind. I shared with a friend how utterly disrespected I felt by her sudden intrusion. I even joked, "I wanted to call her a baldheaded hoe, but I do NOT want the smoke!" Grief is already enough; I don't need the anxiety that comes with wrestling her, or worse, adding anything or anyone else to grieve, so I'm just going to zip it, lock it, and put it in my pocket. Quietly, I'm allowing grief to do what she does without beating myself up about it. Because here's the thing: sometimes we are way too hard on ourselves.

Grief, breakups, failures—these are all things we have to grieve. Take your time. Lean into it. Let grief teach her lessons. She doesn't come empty-handed; she carries wisdom, though it often comes wrapped in sorrow. If we can remember to give ourselves the grace to feel what we feel—without shame or excuses—we might discover the beauty in her lessons.

On the days when grief feels unbearable, lean on your village. Send up a smoke signal if you have to, but let them know what you need. It could be words of comfort or simply someone to sit with you in the stillness. Grief isn't linear, nor is it predictable. But as we navigate her storms, we grow stronger, wiser, and more compassionate—both toward ourselves and others. So, if today is a hard day, lean in, learn, and give yourself permission to just be. You're not alone in this.

Stages of Aging: The Unfiltered Chronicles

As I sit here, reflecting on my journey through the inevitable stages of aging, I can't help but wonder: where are the resources for this phase of life? We've got What to Expect When You're Expecting and Parenting for Dummies, but where's Aging for Dummies or How to Navigate Your Check Engine Light After 40? Honestly, a little guidance would've saved me from the roller coaster I've been on, starting with my annual checkup in January 2023.

At 47, I strolled into the doctor's office feeling fine, not knowing that I was about to have my whole existence questioned. The nurse started with the usual routine, but then her questions took a sharp left turn. "Shortness of breath? Chest pains?" she asked casually. I stared at her, dumbfounded. "Is this because I'm 47? Y'all didn't ask me this when I was 46!" My mind spiraled—was I suddenly church-mother old? Were those strawberry candies with the mysterious filling about to start showing up in my purse? (Side note: has anyone ever seen those candies in a store?) As the nurse continued her interrogation about gout, high blood pressure, and diabetes, the kicker came: "It's time to schedule your routine colonoscopy." I felt like I'd been sucker-punched. But it didn't stop there. During the exam, the doctor dropped a bombshell. "Did you know your left ear is infected?" she asked. "Excuse me, what?! I'm a whole adult! What am I, a toddler? First, you're talking chest pains, and now I have a childish ear infection? This ain't adding up!"

A few weeks later, my knee started betraying me. After several near face-plants, I found myself in front of an orthopedic surgeon. He shyly suggested a knee replacement, probably anticipating my resistance. At that point, I was ready to sign up for anything that would let me walk up the stairs to my room at night without crawling. I imagined myself post-surgery with knees like Megan Thee Stallion, strutting my stuff and living my best life. First, I had to get clearance for surgery. That meant a chest X-ray, an EKG, and what felt like a million other tests. I was so stressed one day that I failed the EKG. FAILED. Turns out, forgetting an important task at work while heading to my appointment doesn't pair well with heart monitoring. After a referral to a cardiologist, I was told my EKG was fine, but I'd need a stress echocardiogram. "We'll do the bike version to save your knee," the doctor said.

Fast forward to the test day. I walked into the room, and there it was: a ten-speed bike seat attached to an exam table. My mouth hit the floor. They strapped me to the table like I was on a Six Flags ride, hooked me up to every monitor known to man, and rubbed my chest with—wait for it—sandpaper. "Sandpaper? Really?" I asked the nurse. She calmly explained it was to remove moisture for the EKG leads. "Girl, you just added moisture with iodine and alcohol pads!" But I digress. Then came the main event. I had to pedal fast enough to keep the monitor between 55 and 60 while the resistance increased every two minutes. At the same time, I had to turn to the left, suspend myself with my barely-there arm strength, and breathe in, hold, and breathe out every 30 seconds for the echo. Oh, and did I mention the blood pressure monitoring every two minutes? I was pedaling, panting, singing the Rocky theme song, and planning the number of times I'd go upside my doctor's head at the follow-up.

As I write this, I'm laughing at the chaos of it all, but aging is no joke. Some mornings, my body aches from doing absolutely nothing. Other days, I'm drenched in night sweats and waking up a dozen times to pee. And then there's the looming fear: What if I die suddenly and leave my family? It's a trauma response, I know, but it's real. Here's the truth: aging is a wild ride. It's scary, unpredictable, and humbling, but it's also a reminder that we're alive, still in the game, still capable of laughing through the madness. After my knee replacement surgery, I plan to do my part to stay healthy, but until then, I'll keep leaning on prayer and humor to get me through.

To everyone on this journey with me: give yourself grace. Let's face the challenges with laughter, faith, and determination. When the road gets tough, let's remind ourselves that aging, with all its quirks, is a privilege. Here's to finding joy in every stage—and to never, ever giving up.

The Glorious Homegoing of Ta-Knee-Sha Knee-Shay
2023

For 46 years, she had been faithful. Through the thick and the thin, the fast and the slow, the pop, lock, and drop it, Ta-Knee-Sha Knee-Shay carried me. However, all good things must come to an end, and her time had come. My right knee had finally put in her two-week notice, and there was no convincing her to stay. So, instead of just letting her go quietly, I did what any rational person would do—I threw her a full-on homegoing service.

Now, let me tell you, I didn't just wake up one day and decide to be dramatic about this. No, no. This was years in the making. Ta-Knee-Sha had seen things. She had run from dogs, escaped from bulls, and climbed more trees than a squirrel with an adrenaline problem. Growing up in the country, you don't just *walk* anywhere—you *run*, leap, and *dodge*. Baby, Ta-Knee-Sha did it all.

In her prime, she was a force. She could drop it low when *Juvenile* said, "Girl, you look good, won't you back that thang up." Oh, and backed it up I did—until the Lord found me. That's when Ta-Knee-Sha transitioned from the club to the church, and let me tell you, she ran those pews like an Olympic sprinter chasing a gold medal in Jesus' name. She carried me in shouts, praise breaks, and Holy Ghost two steps that left ushers fanning me back to life.

But lately, Ta-Knee-Sha had been acting up. She refused to bend properly. She creaked like an old porch swing. She locked up at the most inconvenient moments—one time, right in the middle of a testimony when I was about to take off running. It was then that I knew…her time was near. So, for one last week, I gave her the send-off she deserved. Every night, I danced for her. I spun, dipped, and even attempted one last *back that thang up* (strictly for historical purposes, of course). And on the eve of surgery, we gathered for The Official Celebration of Life for Sister Ta-Knee-Sha Knee-Shay.

My friends showed up dressed in their best church attire, tambourines in hand. We had praise and worship, a eulogy, and a full-on testimony service where we reminisced on all the times she had come through for me. The highlight? When my best friend got up and read from "The Book of Kneesiastes," Chapter 4, Verse 2: *And lo, the knee that once ran, shall run no more. The knee that once bent shall bend no longer. But verily, a new knee shall arise in her place, and she shall be stronger than before.*

We shouted. We cried. We laid hands (gently, of course). And then, we said our final goodbyes. Surgery day came, and Ta-Knee-Sha Knee-Shay was officially no more. In her place was a shiny new titanium knee, fresh out of the factory and ready for action. But the story doesn't end there—oh no because I had made a promise. I told my family that as soon as I was released from the hospital, I would send them a video of me twerking my way to the car and twerking into the house—walker and all. And did I deliver? You BET I did.

There I was, my walker decked out in purple tulle, the nurse looking on in what I can only assume was a mixture of admiration and confusion as I gave my first post-op twerk to freedom. Was it graceful? No. Did my family scream in laughter for hours? Yes. And was it worth every ounce of effort? Absolutely.

So now, as I embark on this journey with my brand-new knee (who I may or may not name *Neecie*), I walk—or rather, twerk—forward into this new chapter of my life. And if you ever wonder if I'll be back to running through church, just wait until this physical therapy is over. Because when I shout this time, baby, I won't just be running—I'll be running on titanium.

Rest in peace, Ta-Knee-Sha Knee-Shay. You were loved. You were cherished. You were slightly problematic, but you were mine.

And now, we *are back at it.*

A Home Built on Faith, Family, and Perseverance
(2024)

Saying goodbye to Ta-Knee-Sha Knee-Shay was not just about parting ways with a failing knee—it was the end of an era. She had carried me through everything: running from dogs, dodging bulls, climbing trees, dancing like nobody was watching, and shouting through church pews like the Spirit had a hand on my back. But as much as I honored her with a full-blown homegoing service—complete with praise, worship, and a eulogy fit for a knee that had genuinely been through it all—I knew something greater was coming. Little did I know that just 10 days post-op, as I hobbled onto a construction site with a walker wrapped in purple tulle, I would be stepping into the biggest blessing of my life.

I always believed in miracles, but I never imagined I would be living in one. I was denied when I first applied for a home through the partnership between the City of Marietta, Marietta City Schools, and Habitat for Humanity. My heart sank, but God whispered to me, "This is for you." I had no idea how, but I knew I had to keep pushing. With a pounding heart, I picked up the phone and called the office, praying that I wouldn't sound like I had lost my mind. The representative agreed to take another look at my documents, and I held my breath. Long story short, God made a way. My new Pop-Up Coffee Shop helped me qualify, and once I was approved, we applied for a community grant. The community rallied around the project, and suddenly, businesses wanted to be part of something bigger—helping build homes for service employees like me.

Then came June 10, 2023—a date I will never forget. Just 10 days post-op from my knee replacement surgery, I showed up at the building site with my husband, Kelcey, on my walker, determined to be part of my own miracle. I was helped onto the foundation, and with shaky hands, I hammered in the first nail. The moment was surreal. The mayor, fire chief, school superintendent, principal, HR director, and countless city officials were there to raise the walls—literally and figuratively. My family and my MMS community showed up in full force, volunteering to build, paint, plant, and most importantly, pray.

It was on that site that I met D'Ana and Tracey, two other women benefiting from this program. We became family from the moment we locked eyes. Our bond was instant, sealed under the safety tent as D'Ana—without hesitation—gave me my heparin injection like we had been doing this for years. That's when I knew this wasn't just a house but the foundation of something much greater.

The dedication day arrived, and as I stood in front of the completed house, surrounded by everyone who had poured their hearts and hands into this build, I tried to speak—but the weight of gratitude was too much. My sweet Mama Shelia opened in prayer, voices echoed with speeches, gifts were given, and I stood there, overwhelmed by the sheer love that had built these walls. Then it happened—the tears I had been holding finally broke free. The Spirit of God wrapped around me in such a sweet embrace that I couldn't recover. Jamorad stepped in and led the closing prayer as everyone gathered around, holding me up—just as they had throughout this journey.

On September 25, 2023, we closed on our home. But the miracles didn't stop there. When Kelcey and I arrived, we were shocked into silence (which, as you know, is rare for me, Honey!). iThink Financial had come in and FULLY FURNISHED our home—every room, down to the washer and dryer, carefully chosen in our favorite colors and styles. And as if that weren't enough, they handed us a check for $500 to start our new chapter. That night, we slept in our new home, and I slept in peace for the first time in a long time.

Fast-forward to 2025, and our home is more than just a place to live—it's a place where life happens. We've had our vow renewal in the backyard, hosted a luau, thrown countless cookouts, and turned our space into an after-school haven for teachers. We planted and tended to our first full garden, watching it flourish just as we have. The house is lived in, filled with laughter, love, and memories in the making.

We are finally home.

Imposter Syndrome: My Reluctant Co-Pilot

It's been a minute since I've put pen to paper—or fingers to keyboard, if we're being modern. Life has been a whirlwind of busyness, in the best way possible, yet still, there's been this nagging voice in the background whispering doubts. Imposter Syndrome, my unwanted co-pilot, has been riding shotgun, questioning every idea I've had for months.

"What's so great about your story?" it sneers.
"Why would anyone care to read about your life?" it taunts.
"Are you really that special?" it jabs.

For a while, I let those whispers turn into an echo chamber. It's funny how the same mind that can encourage and uplift others can sometimes betray you, convincing you that your voice isn't enough, that your story isn't worth telling. Here's what I'm starting to remember and speak to myself—and it's something I hope you remember, too. Your story is always worth telling.

Whether it's about teaching middle schoolers how to manage their emotions while wrangling your own, raising six kids who think you're some combination of cool, quirky, and slightly embarrassing, or being Shooby to five grandbabies who light up your world—your life is full of stories that matter. Whether it's about navigating life with your husband, Kelcey, who makes PawPaw look like a superhero, or helping co-teachers and students find their footing after rocky starts, your words can inspire.

You've been through the trenches. From the heartbreak of grief to the overwhelming joy of seeing students or your own kids overcome obstacles, you've learned, grown, and loved fiercely. That's what makes your story special: it's real. It's full of humor, raw emotion, and moments that make others feel less alone. So what if Imposter Syndrome wants to tag along? Buckle it in the backseat and let it watch as you shine. You're Methany Thornton: a teacher, a coach, a mother, a grandmother, a plant-loving, coffee-drinking, joy-sharing, Jesus-following, Wonder Woman of a woman. You've been called to pour into others, and writing is one of the ways you do that.

I mean, think about it. People love your stories. They laugh, cry, and sometimes snort their coffee while reading about your escapades (the stress echo and Michael Jackson autograph story). Your words heal, encourage, and entertain because they're uniquely you. And here's the truth: not everyone will get it. Not everyone will see your light or understand your purpose. But the ones who need it? They'll cling to your words like a lifeline. You'll remind them they're not alone, that their struggles are valid, and that laughter is often the best medicine.

So, my challenge to you—and everyone reading—is this: don't let Imposter Syndrome steal your joy. Write the story. Share your heart. Be vulnerable. Someone out there is waiting for your words, and trust me, they matter more than you know. You're awesome, Methany, and no whisper of doubt can take that away. Keep writing. The world needs your light.

Menopause:
The Mysterious Club Nobody Warned Us About
(2024)

     If there's one thing I've learned recently, it's that menopause feels like a secret club you're unwillingly inducted into, complete with a hazing process so bizarre that you question your very existence. One day, you're casually living life, enjoying your morning coffee, and the next, you're ripping off your sweater in the middle of a meeting, fanning yourself with your notebook while praying nobody notices the sweat pooling in places you didn't know could sweat. Welcome to Menopause: The Club Nobody Told You About.

The Unspoken Struggle

     Here's the thing about menopause—no one talks about it. It's as if there's a global conspiracy among women over 40 to let you flounder in hormonal chaos without a shred of warning. Mood swings? They're your new emotional rollercoaster. Night sweats? You'll wake up wondering if you swam laps in your sleep. Hot flashes? You'll feel like a human lava lamp, lighting up with no warning…an inferno burning from the inside out. Let's not even get started on the headaches, dry mouth, or those delightful moments when you suddenly feel like snapping at someone because they dared to breathe too loudly.

Breaking the Silence

Why are we suffering in silence? Why aren't we sharing our stories, our tips, or even just a comforting laugh over how ridiculous it all is? Enough is enough. Menopause doesn't have to be a lonely battle. In fact, it shouldn't be. We're in this together, sisters, and it's time we start acting like it. Here's an idea: start your menopause squad. Gather your friends and create a menopause support group. No, I'm not talking about a stiff, clinical meeting with PowerPoints and pamphlets (though if that's your thing, go for it).
I'm talking about wine nights (or tea if you're in the middle of a dry mouth crisis), pajama parties, or even group chats where you can vent about your latest meltdown over mismatched socks. Share your tips, your laughs, and yes, even your tears.

Speaking Your Truth

Write It Out. If you're a writer—or even if you're not—consider journaling about your experiences. Writing can be a therapeutic way to process the madness. Who knows? Maybe your menopause musings will turn into a blog, a book, or a viral TikTok series. The world needs your wit, wisdom, and raw honesty.

Talk It Out. Do you feel like sharing your menopause saga with a broader audience? Start a podcast! You can call it Menopause and Mimosas or Hot Flash Confessions. Invite guests, share stories, and turn your experiences into entertainment and education for women everywhere. Trust me, there are plenty of us who'd love to listen and even be interviewed while dousing ourselves in ice water.

Laugh It Off. Humor is one of the best weapons against the insanity of menopause. It's not just about surviving—it's about thriving in the chaos. Did you throw your keys in the fridge again? Laugh. Did you yell at the toaster for burning your bagel? Laugh. Did you strip down to your bra in the middle of dinner because a hot flash hit you like a freight train? Laugh.

A Word of Encouragement

Menopause doesn't mean you're losing yourself; it means you're transitioning into a new chapter. Yes, it's messy and unpredictable, but it's also a chance to embrace your strength, your humor, and your resilience. You've tackled so much in life—this is just another mountain to climb, albeit one that's covered in sweat and mood swings.

Ladies, let's stop treating menopause like it's taboo. Talk about it. Laugh about it. Create spaces where we can vent, cry, and cheer each other on. Whether it's a local support group, a podcast, or a hilarious meme, your voice matters. Let's normalize this stage of life so the next generation doesn't have to go through it feeling as lost as we sometimes do.

Remember: even on your sweatiest, moodiest, most chaotic days, you're not alone. You're strong. You're amazing. And you're in the hottest club (literally) on the planet. Cheers to you, menopause warrior. Let's get through this together— one hot flash at a time.

Healing in the Hands of a Stranger
(2025)

After moving, I still needed to find my footing in so many ways—new home, new surroundings, new challenges. What weighed most on my mind was the way menopause had been slowly taking over my body and emotions. The hot flashes, the mood swings, the sleepless nights—everything felt out of control, and I knew I needed help.

One of my closest friends, sensing my struggle, recommended her doctor. I had heard so many stories of women struggling to find the right care, but I trusted my friend's judgment and made the appointment. When I sat in front of the doctor, I felt so exposed. I explained my symptoms, trying to maintain some composure, but the tears kept welling up in my eyes. I would take a deep breath and try to push them back, not wanting to show vulnerability, but I could feel it rising. Every word I said felt like a weight being lifted, but at the same time, the gravity of it all was too much.

She listened. Really listened. And then she asked me about stress. I told her about everything—my family dynamics, the shifts in my life, the recent whirlwind of discovering the truth about my biological father through AncestryDNA. If you've followed my journey, you know how much that revelation turned everything upside down. I was already balancing so many emotional storms, and menopause was just piling on top of it all.

Then, with a calm voice, she looked at me, and I swear, she saw right through me. I wasn't just a patient to her. She saw the anger, the exhaustion, the deep hurt I hadn't fully acknowledged myself. She handed me a tissue, not in pity, but in understanding, and then... she read me for filth. She told me that just because people age doesn't mean they mature, and that sometimes, we learn how to do things by watching others do them wrong. She said I was angry—and that I had every right to be. She told me she was proud of me for doing the hard work to heal, but that healing wouldn't come without help, without numbing the pain a little so that I could move forward properly. In that moment, I crumbled. The tears that had been fighting their way to the surface finally came rushing out, a complete mess of emotions that I couldn't hold back anymore.

What she said next—what she did next—changed everything. She looked me in the eyes, and with such sincerity, she affirmed me. A total stranger, who had only just met me, took the time to tell me that I was kind, intelligent, strong, compassionate, and yes—A GOOD MOM AND WIFE. In that moment, she said exactly what I needed to hear, that kind of raw truth. It was as though she saw the best parts of me, even when I couldn't see them for myself. I finally pulled it together, wiped my tears, and left her office with a sense of peace I hadn't known in a long time. The next day, I took my first pill, and almost immediately, I felt a shift. It wasn't magic, but there was a small sense of relief—a pause in the chaos.

I found my friend who had recommended the doctor and, with a laugh through my tears, I asked, "Girl, why you didn't tell me that lady was going to have me in there in shambles?" She laughed, pulled me into a hug, and just let me be for a moment.

It's been seven days on the medicine now. I have to double up tomorrow, and I can feel the anticipation. Here's what I know for sure—I'm doing better. I'm laughing more, if that's even possible. If you know me, you know laughter is my oxygen. It's who I am, and with all that's been going on, the last few days have been filled with more of it…more joy, more peace, more laughter. As I take this next step in my healing process, I'll remember the woman who saw me, really saw me, and gave me the gift of affirmation when I needed it most. Pray for me, y'all. I'm on a journey, and I'm grateful that I am not walking it alone.

The Unexpected Journey: My AncestryDNA Story
(2024)

For most of my life, I believed I knew exactly who I was and where I came from. My identity was stitched together by the stories my family told, the man I grew up calling "Dad," and the memories tucked into our photo albums. It was a certainty I never thought to question. But as my 49th birthday approached, something shifted—a stirring in my spirit, a whisper that there was more to my story than I had ever imagined. In July 2024, I decided to answer the call that had been tugging at me. I ordered an AncestryDNA kit. It felt like a small step in an effort to explore the roots of my heritage and maybe uncover a few surprises to share with my children and grandchildren. When the kit arrived, I followed the instructions, spit into the little tube, sealed it, and sent it off, feeling a mix of curiosity and anticipation. Little did I know, I was opening the door to a life-changing revelation.

The Results That Changed Everything

By September 2024, my results arrived in my inbox. My heart raced as I clicked the link and watched the colorful map of my heritage unfold. I smiled as I saw the rich tapestry of my ancestry: I smiled at the rich tapestry of my ancestry, deeply rooted in West Africa with **Nigeria (32%)**, **Mali (16%)**, and other regions like **Cameroon**, **Senegal**, and **Ivory Coast & Ghana** prominently represented. Additional traces of **Central and Eastern Bantu Peoples** and even **Mainland Southeast Asia** added depth, while European lineage from **England & Northwestern Europe**, **Germanic Europe**, and **Ireland** rounded out my diverse heritage. Each percentage and region told a story, connecting me to a history that spanned continents.

I had taken the test hoping to find out I was Nigerian, Puerto Rican, and Cuban, imagining a vibrant blend of cultural identities. While Puerto Rican and Cuban ancestry didn't appear, my Nigerian roots shone brightly, anchoring me to a heritage that felt both familiar and deeply affirming. Amidst the celebration of these discoveries, another piece caught my attention—a section labeled **"DNA Matches."** There it was: not one name did I recognize under the paternal side. There wasn't anyone I could explain, and my heart sank. I blinked at the screen, rereading the names and relationships. There was one relative who had shown up in my DNA matches that should have matched with both sides but did not. They only matched with my maternal side. This was extremely significant. Suddenly, the narrative I had lived for 48 years began to unravel.

The Truth Unfolds

After some initial hesitation, I reached out to several of the DNA matches. The responses were kind, open, and eager to connect. They revealed a truth I never expected to hear: the man I had known as my father was not biologically my dad. It was a revelation that left me reeling. For 48 years, I had lived one version of my story, and in an instant, everything shifted. But even in the midst of my shock, I felt God's peace nudging me forward. This wasn't just about uncovering the truth; it was about stepping into the fullness of who I was always meant to be.

Determined to learn more, I began piecing together my biological father's identity using the DNA matches and connections on the Ancestry app. This part of the journey was nothing short of miraculous, and I couldn't have done it alone. Special thanks to April Harris, Kita Gardner, Shaniqua Woods, Brenda Copeny-Johnson, Pula Jones, Helena Shobe, and Janara Windmon for guiding me through this process. Their support, expertise, and encouragement were invaluable as I unraveled the threads of my lineage and uncovered the man who was truly my father.

A New Chapter

Meeting some of my newfound family members was a profoundly emotional experience. They welcomed me with open arms, sharing stories about my biological father—his humor, his passions, his essence. For the first time, I began to see reflections of myself in someone I had never known. There was healing in hearing those stories, in being embraced by people who had been a missing piece of my life's puzzle. As I prepared for my 49th birthday, I felt a deep need to share this journey. I decided to post one picture and one reflection each day leading up to my birthday, culminating in the revelation of this life-altering truth. Each post was a testament to God's faithfulness, my family's love, and the beauty of discovering who I really am.

Reflections on Identity

This journey has taught me that identity is not static—it evolves with every discovery, every connection, and every step of faith. I've learned that the truth can be painful, but it can also be the key to healing. Through this process, God reminded me that every piece of my story—no matter how unexpected—was part of His plan for my life. For anyone contemplating a similar journey, I offer this encouragement:

1. Be Open to the Unexpected: The truth might challenge what you thought you knew, but it can also bring clarity and peace.
2. Lean on Your Community: Whether it's friends, family, or newfound relatives, surround yourself with people who will support you through the journey.
3. Trust God's Timing: This process is not just about finding answers; it's about allowing God to reveal what you're ready to receive when you're ready to receive it.

A Challenge for You

As I reflect on this season of discovery, I encourage you to ask: What loose ends is God calling you to tie up? Maybe it's a family mystery, a hidden dream, or an unresolved hurt. Whatever it is, step forward with faith. Trust that God's timing is perfect and that He will guide you through every twist and turn. My journey through AncestryDNA wasn't just about uncovering the past; it was about stepping boldly into the future with a fuller understanding of who I am. It's about knowing that every piece of my story—every joy, every heartache, every revelation—is held lovingly in God's hands. To my newfound family, thank you for your love and kindness. To my friends and supporters, thank you for walking this road with me. And to anyone reading this, may you find the courage to seek your own truths, knowing that healing and hope await you on the other side. Here's to embracing the unexpected and discovering the beauty of our shared humanity.

Dear Who I Thought was my Dad,

When I sent off that AncestryDNA kit last July, I didn't expect it to lead me to this moment. By September, I had my results, and with them came a truth that turned my world upside down. Learning that you aren't my biological father was a revelation I never saw coming. It shook everything I thought I knew about myself, about you, and about the foundation of my identity.

I imagined our conversation would be different when I shared the news. I thought you might be angry or defensive, but instead, you surprised me. You weren't angry—you were calm, even consoling. And there I was, weeping uncontrollably, unraveling under the weight of it all. You were the one trying to comfort me, but it only made the emotions more complex. I kept thinking, why do I have to fix their mess, **again?!**

You told me you never suspected this. That you never questioned whether you were my father. Your words felt like a soft landing when I expected jagged edges. But even as you tried to make sense of it alongside me, I was too shaken to confront the deeper wounds. I couldn't find the strength to ask why you treated me like an embarrassment for most of my life…why your absence felt louder than your presence…why I grew up feeling like the broken pieces of your and Mama's choices were mine to carry.

Dear Mama,

I had braced myself for a different kind of response from you. Maybe an explanation, some missing pieces, or even a tearful acknowledgment of how deeply this journey would affect me. But instead, you were indifferent—almost flippant. When I needed understanding, you gave me shrugs. When I asked for answers, you offered silence. And it stung. It stung deeply.

You couldn't give me any information about my biological father, and your reaction felt like a dismissal of the emotional storm I was caught in. I can't pretend that your response didn't hurt, but I also can't stay angry. I'm choosing to believe that your nonchalance was a shield for your own pain—a way of protecting yourself from the weight of what I was uncovering. Even though it left me feeling more alone in this discovery than I ever imagined, I know we've both been shaped by choices that were never easy.

Dear Dad,

I never thought I'd be writing you a letter like this, especially not under these circumstances. For so much of my life, I thought I knew my story, my family, and my place in this world. But then, through the unexpected journey of AncestryDNA, I found you—a truth that answered so many lingering questions about myself yet left me grappling with an ache I didn't know was there.

You've been gone almost five years now, and that reality cuts deep. Knowing who you are has filled in so many gaps in my life—my features, my mannerisms, the pieces of me that never quite fit in the narrative I grew up with. But at the same time, your absence has created a void I don't quite know how to navigate. I find myself wishing I could hear your voice, see your smile, or ask you all the questions swirling in my mind. Who were you? What were your dreams? Would you have been proud to call me your daughter?

Tomorrow, I'll visit your grave for the first time. I don't know exactly what I'm hoping to feel, but I know I'm searching for something—closure, connection, maybe even a sense of peace. I want to believe that, in some way, you'll be there with me, in the quiet moments by your resting place or in the stories shared by the family I've met and will meet as I continue this journey of discovery. I want to feel you in their laughter, their kindness, and their memories of the man you were.

Dad, I wish I had the chance to know you in life, to hear your side of the story, to create memories together, to let you see the person I've become, but I trust that God has a plan for even this part of my journey. Finding you, even after all this time, has been a gift. It has given me the courage to confront the parts of myself I didn't understand and to embrace the truth of who I am. As I stand at your grave tomorrow, I'll say the things I never had the chance to tell you in life: I'm grateful for the pieces of you I carry within me. I'm sad that you are not here because I know life isn't always simple or kind, and I love you, not because of what you could have been, but because of who you were and the part you play in my story.

Your family—our family—has welcomed me with open arms, and I hope through them, I'll feel the warmth of your presence. I hope to honor you by living with the same resilience and strength I imagine you carried. Until we meet again,

Your Daughter, Methany

Reflections

This journey wasn't just about DNA. It was about uncovering truths that have always been there, hidden in plain sight, waiting for the right moment to surface. I've had to reckon with the reality that my heritage carries both darkness and light. Yet, through it all, God's hand has been steady. He has shielded me, guided me, and reminded me that His plans for me are good. For 48 years, I believed a story that wasn't entirely true. Now, I stand in the space where that old narrative ends and a new one begins. It's messy, painful, and filled with questions I may never have answers to. It's also a place of healing, a place where forgiveness is no longer a lofty idea but a necessity.

To anyone else walking this path of unraveling truths and redefining identity: it's okay to weep. It's okay to grieve, and it's okay to ask the hard questions, even if the answers never come. Take your time. Lean into your faith. Above all, remember that the pieces of your story—however fractured they may feel—are still part of a beautiful whole.

With love, forgiveness, and hope…

To My New Family

Where do I even begin? My heart is overflowing with gratitude, love, and awe at how quickly and profoundly you've changed my life. In such a short time, you've opened doors to a part of my story that I never thought I would uncover—my biological father's truth, a truth I've been seeking for 49 years. But this journey has never been about just finding a name or a connection. It's been about discovering *you*—a family I didn't know existed but somehow, I've always needed.

Since we connected, I've felt welcomed, accepted, and loved in a way I'd never expected. You've embraced me with open arms and hearts, offering me a love that's tender and strong. It's the kind of love that fills the gaps in all the places I thought were missing and, in its place, has created something beautiful. You've given me the most precious gift—the gift of family, not just by blood but by choice. Through you, I've learned that family isn't just about genetics; it's about the bond we choose to create, nurture, and protect. I never expected to find this kind of love, yet here it is—proof that God's plans are always greater than we could ever imagine. His hand has been so evident in this journey, and I'm in awe of how He's woven us together, bringing us closer with each passing day.

Thank you all from the depths of my heart for everything you've shown me. You've filled my life with much more than I could have imagined. You've brought me peace in places I didn't even know were unsettled, and you've helped me heal wounds I thought were too deep to touch. Through your love, I've found my worth.

To my sister April, what a joy it has been getting to know you. You've already shown me what sisterhood is supposed to be, and I can't wait to laugh with you, share memories, and spoil you just as every big sister should. Your words, kindness, and encouragement mean the world to me. You've opened my eyes to a whole new understanding of who I am, and I'm so grateful to have you in my life.

To my Aunt Brenda and Aunt Pula, thank you for warmly accepting me. Aunt Brenda, your check-ins, love, and honesty have touched me deeply. The depth of your transparency and love is something I will always treasure. Thank you for connecting me with this beautiful family, and I hope I can spoil you in the same way you've shown me love.

To my cousins Gee Gee, Ni Ni, and Kita, I can't even begin to explain how much it means to have you in my life. Gee Gee, our connection is nothing short of a miracle. Ni Ni and Kita, I'm so thankful for you both and how you helped me to connect the dots to find the missing parts of myself. You have helped fill spaces in my heart that I didn't even know were empty. I can't wait to continue this journey with you all, to grow our bond and create memories together. Our family feels so right, and I know this is only the beginning of something incredibly special.

To Keasha, To Keasha, thank you for being the bridge that led me to this beautiful revelation. Who could have imagined that all our years of working, laughing, and crying together would bring me here? You've played a key role in helping me uncover the truth I've been searching for, and I will forever cherish how you helped me find the missing pieces of my puzzle. I mean, your sister-in-law is my cousin—this is the kind of story that belongs in a movie!

To my cousin, April Harris, thank you for your heartfelt words. I hear you, and I appreciate your perspective so much. I know my journey with my mother hasn't been what I envisioned, but you helped me to understand that life doesn't always give us the perfect hand. What matters most is how we play the hand we've been dealt, and I'm doing my best to play it with grace, faith, and love. Your words about God filling all my voids with the right people have been comforting. I feel His presence in my life and see how He's brought beautiful people like you into my world, helping me heal and find completeness.

I've learned that even in the gaps, God provides. I may not have had the mom I thought I needed, but I have many incredible people, including you, who have shown me love and guidance.

This journey has taught me that our stories—no matter how messy, broken, or beautiful—are worth sharing. Through sharing our stories, we discover who we truly are and who we were always meant to be. Reflecting on all the love and truth that has come into my life, I feel nothing but gratitude. This Christmas was different—not because of the lights or the presents, but because I am finally walking in the fullness of who I am. I've let go of old hurts, doubts, and fears and embraced this new chapter with open arms. Each of you has played an essential part in my healing journey, and I will forever be thankful for that.

I am in awe of how God has brought us together and how He's used each of you to fill the gaps and show me that my story is far from over. You are not just family; you are the answer to prayers I didn't know I was praying. Through you, I've learned that I have no emptiness—only room for more love, connection, and truth.

Thank you for being exactly who you are—beautiful, loving, and full of grace. I can't wait to see where this journey takes us and all the big and small moments we'll share.
I love you all so much, already and always.

With all my heart,

Methany

Real Love and Real Lessons:
A Birthday with Mary J. Blige

My sister bought me tickets to see Mary J. Blige for my birthday, a gift I will never forget. I wanted to honor Mary in the best way I knew how, so I dressed in a "Real Love"-inspired outfit—an oversized Bad Boy jersey, a bodysuit, slouch socks, a black and white cap worn to the back, and combat boots. I was ready.

When we arrived at State Farm Arena, I was excited, but that excitement quickly turned into confusion when I set off the metal detectors. I walked through four times, frustrated, until I remembered: "Neecie"—my titanium knee. I whispered the reason, but the attendant couldn't hear me. Before I knew it, I yelled in front of the crowd, "It's my knee!" Suddenly, everyone looked at me, and we laughed...hysterically!

We were in Section 120, Row V, Seat 10. Our seats were amazing, and I couldn't wait to feel the energy in the air. As soon as the music started, I sang until I was hoarse, danced until my knees had a life of their own, and shouted out to all the fine aunties in my section. In my mind, this wasn't just a concert—it was *my* birthday party. Mario, Ne-Yo, and Mary herself had all come to perform just for me. Every time there was a pause in the music, I shouted, "THANK YOU FOR COMING TO MY PARTY!"

But then, something more profound happened. During one of the moments when Mary was talking to us, I sat down, closed my eyes, and let the music and her words wash over me. Mary shared her story about her father and his struggles with mental health after returning from the Vietnam War. She spoke with such vulnerability, opening her heart about the pain she had carried and the forgiveness she had to find for others and herself. At that moment, I felt like Mary wasn't just singing to us—she was speaking directly to me. She said, "I am that girl, that b*tch, that whoever you want me to be… I am her."

Her words hit me so deeply. She wasn't just a superstar to me; she was a reflection of the strength and resilience that we, as Black women, carry within us daily. Her journey was my journey; her growth was my growth.

For over 33 years, I've been listening to Mary's music—her pain, joy, and realness. Her songs became mine; they made me feel seen in ways I couldn't describe. That night, I knew I wanted to finish my book with a tribute to her—to honor her the way she has honored us with her music and her life.

Mary, thank you for being so unapologetically you. Thank you for showing us that it's okay to be vulnerable, forgive, and always be true to ourselves. Your life and your music have taught me lessons I will carry forever. We love you, Mary, and we're so grateful for everything you've given us. You truly gave us the 411.

Epilogue: Embracing the Journey

Life rarely unfolds the way we expect it to. If someone had told me years ago that I'd be here, writing this book, reflecting on the twists and turns that have shaped me, I would have laughed—or cried, depending on the day. But here I am, at the end of this chapter, holding the weight of everything I've experienced and learned, yet feeling lighter than ever. When I first began this journey, I thought I was just tying up loose ends, unraveling a few mysteries, and documenting some stories to share. But as the pages unfolded, I realized this was about so much more. It was about healing old wounds, rediscovering parts of myself, and learning to love the messy, imperfect beauty of my life. It was about acknowledging the pain, embracing the joy, and finding the courage to face everything in between.

The process of uncovering my past wasn't easy. There were days when grief and anger threatened to overwhelm me, when I questioned my worth, and when I doubted my ability to keep going. But through it all, I held on to my faith, knowing that God was with me, weaving every tear, every laugh, every revelation into a tapestry more intricate and beautiful than I could imagine. And what a tapestry it is. It's woven with the laughter of my grandchildren, the resilience of my children, and the unwavering love of my husband, Kelcey. It's colored by the strength of the women in my family, the lessons my students teach me daily, and the friendships that have sustained me through every storm. It's anchored by the discovery of my biological father, the connection to his family, and the answers I never thought I'd find.

This memoir is not just a collection of stories; it's a celebration of survival, of learning to live fully and authentically in the face of life's uncertainties. It's a testament to the power of forgiveness—not just for others, but for myself. It's a reminder that every step, even the painful ones, is part of a journey worth taking. As I close this book, I find myself reflecting on one of my favorite scriptures: "He makes everything beautiful in its time" (Ecclesiastes 3:11). It's a truth I've seen unfold in my life, over and over again. The pieces that once seemed broken have come together in ways I couldn't have imagined. The unanswered questions have led to discoveries that deepen my understanding of myself and my place in the world. And the love I've given and received along the way has reminded me that I am never alone.

But through all of this—every tear, every laugh, every revelation—I keep coming back to one thing. I just want to be her. The woman who knows her worth and stands firm in it. The woman who laughs loudly, loves fiercely, and forgives freely. The woman who embraces the fullness of who she is, flaws and all, and doesn't apologize for the space she takes up in this world. I always want to be her—the woman who chooses joy even in the face of pain, who leans on her faith to carry her through the storm, and who looks in the mirror and sees someone beautifully made. Not perfect, but whole. Not without scars, but stronger because of them. Not trying to prove anything to anyone—just being herself. That's the woman I am becoming, step by step, day by day. And if this journey has taught me anything, it's that becoming her is the most beautiful, messy, and rewarding adventure of all.

With all my heart, I just want to be her.

Methany Thornton

A Prayer

Lord,

As we turn the final page of this book, I thank You for every reader who has walked this journey with me. Thank You for the laughter that reminds us of Your joy, the love that reflects Your heart, and the lessons that deepen our understanding of who we are and who You've called us to be.
I pray for each person holding this book in their hands. Bless them in their own stories, Lord—stories still being written, full of chapters yet to unfold. Please give them the courage to face the unknown, the strength to rise after every fall, and the hope to see beauty amid the chaos. Let them remember that they, too, are storytellers with lives that inspire, uplift, and bring light to the world.

Amen.

A Challenge

To you, dear reader, I offer this challenge: Live boldly. Love deeply. Learn from every moment and laugh until your sides ache. Seek the lessons hidden in the messiness of life, and don't be afraid to share your story— because someone out there needs to hear it.

When I shared my AncestryDNA journey on social media, some thought it was too personal or risky. They didn't understand why I would lay my heart bare for all to see. But I listened to what my heart and faith told me to do, and the response was humbling. So many people reached out, inspired by my vulnerability, to share their own stories of discovery. Some found the courage to connect with new family members because I was brave enough to take the first step.

Let that be a reminder: your bravery can inspire others. Your story can spark healing, connection, and hope in someone else's life, no matter how messy or uncertain. Know that this is not the end but a pause in the rhythm of what's still to come. I hope that as you close this book, you'll feel empowered to keep turning the pages of your own life with excitement, faith, and a sense of purpose.

The best stories always leave us longing for more, and I promise there will be more to share. Until then, may you walk in grace, guided by love and sustained by hope.

Love Always,

Methany